Disnarration

The Unsaid Matters

Disnarration

The Unsaid Matters

Sudha Shastri

Orient BlackSwan

ORIENT BLACKSWAN PRIVATE LIMITED

Registered Office
3-6-752 Himayatnagar, Hyderabad 500 029, Telangana, India
Email: centraloffice@orientblackswan.com

Other Offices
Bengaluru, Bhopal, Chennai, Ernakulam, Guwahati,
Hyderabad, Jaipur, Kolkata, Lucknow, Mumbai,
New Delhi, Noida, Patna, Vijayawada

First published 2016

ISBN 978 81 250 6238 7

Typeset in Georgia 10/12.5 by
MacroTex Solutions, Chennai 600 091

022419

22012016

Printed in India at
Rakmo Press,
Greater Noida

Published by
Orient Blackswan Private Limited
1/24 Asaf Ali Road
New Delhi 110 002
Email: delhi@orientblackswan.com

Contents

Editor's Acknowledgements

This volume comprises the select proceedings of a refereed conference on Disnarration, called *'The Road Not Taken': Explorations in Narrative Refusals, Disnarration, and Counterfactual Histories*, that I had organised at the Indian Institute of Technology (IIT) Bombay, Mumbai, from 1–2 March 2013.

I gratefully acknowledge the financial assistance I received for organizing this conference from the Industrial Research and Consultancy Centre (IRCC), IIT Bombay, as well as the Department of Humanities and Social Sciences (HSS), IIT Bombay. This funding enabled me to offer accommodation to participants at the IIT Guest House, and cover expenses of the conference. In this regard I place on record my thanks to Professor Devang Khakhar, Director, IIT Bombay; Professor A K Suresh, then Dean of Faculty Affairs, IIT Bombay; and Professor K Narayanan, then Head of the Department of HSS, IIT Bombay.

Further, I thank my colleagues from the department, Professors Paulomi Chakraborty, Pravesh Jung Golay and Ratheesh Radhakrishnan for helping me to plan and hold this conference.

I am also grateful to Nisha Viswanathan and Professor Siby K. George for helping me especially in those tiny matters of detail that can make or mar a book; and am deeply obliged to Dr Madhavi Menon, Associate Publisher, Orient BlackSwan for her diligence, patience and encouragement to me in my moments of editorial panic.

Sudha Shastri
Mumbai
18 December 2015

Editor's Acknowledgements

Introduction

1

Most of the papers in this volume (all but one) were presented at a refereed conference on disnarration held on 1–2 March 2013, at the Indian Institute of Technology Bombay, titled 'The Road Not Taken'. The impulse towards this conference came from the recognition that despite the notion of 'the disnarrated' having exciting theoretical implications for narrative studies, not much attention has been devoted to it in the intervening years since Gerald Prince published his essay 'The Disnarrated'.[1]

The 1980s had begun to see an extension of the horizon of narratological studies. No longer was narratology confined by structuralism; it also stretched to include narratives that were not strictly literary, and to deploy theories and reading tools from other disciplines. This was the time that Gerald Prince brought forth his concept of disnarration.

Densely packed with idea and reasoning, Prince's essay approaches its topic via the notion of tellability: why is a certain event or sequence of events considered worth narrating? What makes it worth telling? In answering this question, Prince identifies the following limits to narrative tellability. Social convention could be one: recounting certain events can constitute transgression akin to taboo in certain societies, of which a familiar example is the description of sex in Victorian literature; narratorial knowledge could be another: what of events that lie beyond the narrator's knowledge? How is s/he to narrate what s/he does not know? Narrative value is yet another threshold: what if something is not interesting enough to narrate? Prince proposes the categories of the un- or non-narratable and the un- or non-narrated to explain the foregoing limits, which determine choices and decisions regarding the narration or non-narration of certain events in a narrative. Some of these choices could be determined also by genre,[2] context and authorial preferences. Prince's rigorous definition of 'the disnarrated' is thus marked by the elimination of competing narratological ideas like the non-narratable and the non-narrated. Citing the Russian Formalist Shklovsky's notion of negative comparison, where the point of comparison is either absent or refuted or merely hypothetical, Labov's theory of comparators of unrealised events and Marie-Laure Ryan's '*virtual* embedded narratives' (Prince 3, emphasis added), Prince establishes the context of his own contribution to the understanding of narratives.

His essay further illustrates the various ways in which the disnarrated can manifest itself in a narrative, with a vast spectrum of samples: 'terms, phrases, and passages that consider what did not or does not take place . . . whether they pertain to the narrator and his or her narration . . . or to one of the characters and his or her actions', and includes 'alethic expressions of impossibility or unrealized possibility, deontic expressions of observed prohibition, epistemic expressions of ignorance, ontologic expressions of nonexistence, purely imagined worlds, desired worlds, or intended worlds, unfulfilled expectations, unwarranted beliefs, failed attempts, crushed hopes, suppositions and false calculations, errors and lies, and so forth' (Prince 3).

As the above array indicates, the scope of the disnarrated is vast. Prince's comprehensive cataloguing offers a fertile ground for new readings, and perhaps more significantly, new ways of reading or even re-reading existing narratives, pointing to huge additions in scholarship. It is this opportunity for revisiting texts that the conference on disnarration – 'The Road Not Taken' – sought to address through the papers that were selected for presentation.[3]

But what is the role of the disnarrated in a narrative? Prince negotiates this critical 'so what' question almost immediately after defining it, with a seemingly counter-intuitive observation that 'the disnarrated is clearly not essential to narrative' since it is confined to the realm of what does not eventually, come to transpire. Prince's stated reason for focusing nevertheless on what does not happen within a paradigm where what happens ('assurance') (4) is the norm, is the frequent appearance of the disnarrated within narratives in the form of speculation or hypothesis, prompting him therefore to ask why.[4] This question also enables self-reflexivity in reading, which Prince acknowledges towards the end of his essay by remarking that disnarration can work on the level of story as well as discourse (6).

The effects of disnarration are multiple, as Prince points out. One is a retardation of plot, in much the way authorial musings or descriptive passages in a novel can slow the pace of reading. This could constitute a story-level consequence of disnarration. From another perspective, disnarration foregrounds the question of narrative logic, when the narrator either explicitly or implicitly demonstrates the various trajectories that the plot of the narrative could have taken, and the reason for the choice of the trajectory it eventually did. Because of its positing, at least in theory, alternate and parallel worlds in narrative, worlds which are not necessarily mutually exclusive, the disnarrated can find itself niched within postmodern writing.

Prince observes that 'the explicitly metafictional text resorts to the disnarrated mainly on the level of discourse in order to insist on its own artificiality' (6). John Fowles' *The French Lieutenant's Woman* is an early example where the narrator tosses a coin to decide the course of the narrative; and provides two endings, which in the 'real' world, can only be mutually exclusive. There is a 'happy' ending consisting of the union of the lovers, and a 'sad' ending where they part, and the reader is ostensibly given the freedom to choose the ending of her preference. Although the sad ending, coming after the happy one, exerts itself as the final one by virtue of conventional modes of reading,[5] the fact that both are competing endings takes the reader's focus away from the mimetic world of story into the world of its crafting.

The question of narrative logic is another concern of disnarration, made explicit in postmodern texts.[6]

The implications of Prince's theory are immense. In her study Laura Karttunen enlarges the scope of the disnarrated to understand how negatives implicate a wider cultural context within which they make sense, thus taking the idea of disnarration ahead conceptually without necessarily restricting the definition to narratives. When she states, for instance, that in 'reacting to previous texts . . . and imagining alternative histories (what could have been) postcolonial literature involves the disnarrated almost by definition', she is focusing on the value of negatives for 'conveying presuppositional information' (425). Here we have an instance of how disnarration works over and beyond 'just' stories.

2

A famous novelistic example of foregrounding the disnarrated would be Jane Austen's *Northanger Abbey* (1818), in which the gothic novel is present as an ironic subtext, but eventually rejected in favour of the realistic narrative that Austen is invested in. The parodic background of *Northanger Abbey* effects the disnarration; a potential narrative trajectory constructed from the conventions of the gothic genre is apparently predicted; but this outcome is then withheld or as Prince would say, 'disnarrated'.

Catherine Morland, the naïve heroine of Austen's novel loses her perspective as well as common sense on account of being an avid consumer of gothic fiction, in particular, of Mrs Radcliffe's novel *The Mysteries of Udolpho*, with absurd results. In its disnarration of gothic fiction, *Northanger Abbey* also encourages the reader to consider the gothic genre of fictional representation with a predetermined attitude, by deploying the tools of parody.

Northanger Abbey is parodic not just through the regular means of exaggeration and caricature that can turn horror into farce, but also on account of being situated in a generic context which renders a certain narrative progress, otherwise acceptable, absurd and excessive. Catherine Morland is established negatively, as a heroine against the grain of heroines in fiction in the opening sentence of Austen's novel: 'No one who had ever seen Catherine Morland in her infancy would have supposed her born to be an heroine' (3). Already the narrator is appealing to the reader's recognition of the conventions of constructing a prototypical novelistic heroine. Or take the fourth sentence describing her father, which presupposes the gothic narrative: 'He had a considerable independence besides two good livings—*and he was not in the least addicted to locking up his daughters*' (3, emphasis mine). Here a certain type of literary father is evoked who is derived from the gothic-novel paradigm.

Subsequently in the novel when Catherine is invited to visit Northanger Abbey, her imagination is fired by fanciful ideas stemming from the type of fiction she is addicted to reading. Reminiscent of the gothic novels of Mrs Radcliffe that Catherine passionately reads, there is a chest in the room where she stays in the Abbey, but with several empty drawers which discourage her; until she finds one with an ostensible manuscript in it; alas! Just as she tries to snuff her candle for better light with which to read it, the candle dies. She has to endure a night of suspenseful agony before learning that the 'secret document' as she thought it to be was but an inventory of linen, nothing less sensational (Austen 135 43).[7]

Northanger Abbey's climactic moment of disnarrating the gothic comes when Catherine, finding Henry's father General Tilney to be an autocratic widower, who did not seem to have cared much for his late wife, concludes as follows:

> the probability that Mrs Tilney yet lived, shut up for causes unknown, and receiving from the pitiless hands of her husband a nightly supply of coarse food, was the conclusion *which necessarily followed* . . . . In support of the plausibility of this conjecture, it further occurred to her that the forbidden gallery, in which lay the apartments of the unfortunate Mrs Tilney, must be, as certainly as her memory could guide her, exactly over this suspected range of cells, and the staircase by the side of those apartments of which she had caught a transient glimpse, communicating by some secret means with those cells, might well have favoured the barbarous proceedings of her husband. Down that staircase she had perhaps been conveyed in a state of well-prepared insensibility! (156, emphasis mine).

As readers of this novel know, all of the above fanciful imaginings of Catherine's are discounted by the narrative that ensues, thereby becoming part of what Prince would call the disnarrated.

Furthermore, Henry Tilney chides Catherine for indulging her imagination both excessively as well as unjustly. Significantly enough, the specific detail of an incarcerated wife can be traced back to Mrs Radcliffe's *A Sicilian Romance*, in which the Marquis of Mazzini, in love with another woman, has his wife locked up in a hidden part of his residence for years, until by sheer chance his daughter Julia finds her imprisoned mother.

The example of *Northanger Abbey* also suggests interfaces between disnarration and other narrative practices like intertextuality. Parody, as a form of imitation tending to ridicule, can itself be seen as a form of intertextuality. Arguing from this standpoint, the gothic fiction-genre in general and *A Sicilian Romance* in particular form back-texts enabling an intertextual reading of *Northanger Abbey*. At the same time, gothic fiction and *A Sicilian Romance* also contribute to the disnarration of *Northanger Abbey*. This is made possible by the fact that both disnarration and intertextuality predicate a fissure or rupture in a self-contained narrative to make another text's presence evident.

Intertextuality is typically contingent upon a larger tradition of writing, which makes it possible for a later text to make a reference, overt or otherwise, to an earlier text, whether in veneration, denunciation, or ridicule. The disnarrated on the other hand derives from a speculative, hypothetical alternate, which is implicit in the text itself. Of course, these alternates are predetermined by narrative contexts, conventions and genres, which also lie outside the sphere of the specific text in question.

3

The well-known essay, 'Dream-Children: A Reverie' by Charles Lamb is another case in point of disnarration. Lamb occupies the position of a first-person narrator recounting his childhood to his children, who are assembled around him, listening with rapt attention. The early sections of the narration revolve around his grandmother Field and the holidays that he, as a boy, spent in the huge house in Norfolk where she worked. The narrative then shifts to his recollections of wandering about the great house, its rooms and its gardens, finding

> . . . pleasure in strolling about among the old melancholy-looking yew trees, *or* the firs, and picking up the red berries, and the fir apples, which were good for nothing but to look at—*or* in lying about upon the fresh grass, with all the fine garden smells around me—*or* basking in the orangery, till I could almost fancy myself ripening, too, along with the oranges and the limes in that grateful warmth—*or* in

watching the dace that darted to and fro in the fish pond . . . (emphases added).

The holiday pleasures that Lamb lists in the above passage appear as alternative pursuits through his use of 'or' rather than the inclusive, additive 'and'. While this may merely indicate a stylistic preference, and may not have been intended by the author to suggest that his leisure-interests were mutually exclusive, it does occupy the position of a *mise en abyme*, in which a 'part of a work resembles the larger work in which it occurs' (William Nelles 312);[8] this is made evident when the audience of children, before whom he reminisces, are revealed at the end of the account to be 'dream children', who could have but did not exist, except in the fond fantasies of the narrator. They are the dream-children of the title; shadows of the children he might have had if he had married his love Alice Liddell. Thus, the excerpt above indicates the boy's several amusements in a syntactic suggestion of alternative trajectories, by the deployment of 'or'; which the essay as a whole complements by disclosing at the end that the account itself is an 'alternate' one, rooted not in the world of reality or history, but in speculation.

'Dream-Children' is thus a curious instance of a narrative whose outer frame or context begins with certitude of a certain kind[9] and ends with its negation. The imaginary audience's last words are '"[W]e are nothing; less than nothing, and dreams. We are only what might have been, and must wait upon the tedious shores of Lethe millions of ages before we have existence, and a name"'. Over centuries, Lamb's moving personal account of unrealized love has been upheld as a literary exemplar of melancholic reflection. What has not been remarked is that at the same time, this essay also succeeds as a model of Prince's concept of the 'disnarrated'.

4

The papers read at the conference support the belief that not only is disnarration an 'under-worked' topic, but it also covers a potentially huge space seeking delimiting description. Within Prince's definition of disnarration, it is possible to bring an entire genre like historical fiction under the purview of the 'disnarrated'. However, while the implications of such a reading are exciting, the problem this can pose in terms of demarcating what constitutes the 'disnarrated', is equally weighty, begging the question, 'Is disnarration (just) a different way of reading texts?' And if so, what does it mean to our understanding of literary interpretation? These questions also comprised a challenge we faced in session-formation, where we needed to assign similar-themed papers to a single session. One way in which we worked around this question was by falling back on conventional, accepted rubrics like 'gender', 'postcoloniality', 'race', and even 'genre' (such as film).

The first two essays that follow after the Introduction to this volume formed the basis of the plenary address on each of the two days of the conference. Professor Jasbir Jain's comprehensive and exhaustive essay brings together writers as diverse as Kafka, Manto and Marquez to take the questions of disnarration to vastly different texts. Erasures, fissures, silences and repetitions as representative modes of disnarration are profiled across an enviable corpus of texts, substantiated by the understanding of reality as multiple and changing. Professor Supriya Chaudhuri's paper begins by comparing the notion of exclusion implicit in Prince's concept of disnarration with such compatible classical rhetorical devices as apophasis, which is characterised by inclusion. The point thereby made addresses the question earlier raised as to how far the disnarrated is a way of reading rather than a textual imperative.

Section Two brings together the individual papers on disnarration and specific texts, while simultaneously showcasing the sheer range of disnarrative practices. Locating disnarration within the discourse of gender, Paulomi Chakraborty's paper focuses on the silence around the trauma of the protagonist victim Sutara in Jyotirmoyee Devi's *The River Churning: A Partition Novel*. Chakraborty argues that such silence not only withholds from the characters and the reader the knowledge of the truth, but also from Sutara herself; and that this implicitly reflects a societal code which makes the victim's suffering irrelevant in the larger patriarchal definition of her as 'soiled' rather than 'traumatised'. At another end of the spectrum, Rohit Dutta Roy's paper introduces the disnarrated into the interface of fiction and history. Scrutinising the two historical novels, *Ananda Math* and *Jay Somnath* by Bankimcandra and Munshi respectively, this paper shows how a desired world is projected from revivalist ideology, thereby showcasing the political edge of the disnarrated.

Moving from gender and plot to genre, Vinita Singh and Nisha Viswanathan both read disnarration into film, but in markedly different ways. While analysing one of her primary texts (*Barfi*), Singh gives several instances of the most obvious understanding of what constitutes the disnarrated, such as in the way Shruti fantasises a marriage with Barfi (which did not take place). However it is in the examination of how the disnarrated is *recalled* in terms of what did not happen, that Singh's paper makes a leap into theoretical possibilities. In her paper, Viswanathan finds in disnarration the paradigm to understand the success of Chile's plebiscite against Pinochet in 1988, on which the movie *No* is based. By using relevance theory to make sense of the counter-intuitive working of an advertisement, this paper ties disnarration in with counterfactuality in a nation-building context. The exploratory reach of these papers goes a considerable way not only towards establishing definitive thresholds of disnarration, but also demonstrating specific test cases of what can constitute the disnarrated.

Krishnan Unni in his paper sums it up succinctly when he says that disnarration is both a new as well as requisite mode of textual reading in current times, as it 'proposes a whole range of questions connected to the ways of looking at, explicating and alternate reading of the texts in our time' and 'the need to find discontinuities' in texts. This paper ably locates disnarration in the way in which Sebald creates counter-narratives to prevent one fixed way of looking at the past, and suggestively applies the trope of ruins to memory, especially multiple and plural memories. Postmodernism is in fact one of the more familiar styles within which plural worlds, alternate worlds and simultaneous possibilities belong naturally.

So does native American fiction accommodate plurality, although with a palpably different world-view, as exemplified in two papers in this volume. The compatibility of disnarration with the ideology of multiple realities, none of which is privileged or hierarchised over the others, is projected in David Franklin's paper on Erdrich's novel, *Tracks*, through two competing narrators. Anushka Sen's paper refines this self-reflexively by pointing to the creation of plural story-telling traditions in Thomas King's *Green Grass, Running Water*. Sen extends the theoretical as well as exploratory range of disnarration in her paper by testing it against King's novel, and showing where disnarration can fall short.

Sreya Dutt's paper takes forward the question of the compatibility of the oral narrative with disnarration, by marking competing narrative trajectories in Mario Vargas Llosa's *The Storyteller*. On the one hand, silence between the *hablador* and the Machiguenga community becomes a wall that cannot be breached by documentary-makers who are trying to render them 'rationally', and write them into the mainstream nationalist discourse; on the other is the author's endeavour to imagine a reclusive story-teller of the community from within. The concurrent strands disnarrate each other.

Shinjini Chattopadhyay's paper that brings Auster's *The New York Trilogy* and Genette's formulations regarding author, narrator and character together makes a theoretical addition to the questions coming from disnarration. Lending a metafictional perspective towards genres and generic limits, Chattopadhyay's argument opens detective fiction's disnarrative possibilities outside its mimetic world.

But it is not just postmodern ideological structures that enable reading the disnarrated in a text. Debapriya Basu's essay locates the disnarrated in Anne Dowriche's *The French historie*, a text that is more than four centuries old, thereby showing the relevance as much as the validity of Prince's valuable conceptual tool. Dowriche's poem, set closely in a religiously and politically seething historical period, ostensibly narrates the St Bartholomew's Day massacre but in fact deploys fissures creating spaces of ambivalence, within which the disnarrated makes pointers towards directions that it does not explicitly traverse.

Through this volume, it has been our collective endeavour as scholars and researchers to understand the use of disnarration in our academic reading of texts. The sense of a new tool, not so much in the nature of a formula, as much as a way of grasping structures of creation and meaning, has informed many of the papers in this volume, making possible an excitement even with texts already read and re-read and re-interpreted through literary history. We believe that this is but the beginning of a discursive practice pertaining not just to narratives, but to our view of reality – or in the spirit of disnarration, realities: imagined, re-imagined, constructed, and deconstructed.

Notes

1. Among well-known studies are Marie-Laure Ryan's full-length study 'Possible Worlds, Artificial Intelligence, and Narrative Theory' and Robyn Warhol's work including 'Neonarrative; or, How to Render the Unnarratable in Realist Fiction and Contemporary Film', ''What Might Have Been Is Not What Is': Dickens's Narrative Refusals' and 'Narrative Refusals and Generic Transformation in Austen and James: What Doesn't Happen in *Northanger Abbey* and *Spoils of Poynton*.'
2. Speaking of detective fiction, Prince distinguishes the temporary absence caused by narrative gaps from what constitutes the disnarrated: 'in detective novels, for instance, the possible solutions and false solutions it introduces are contrasted with the real ones' (5). These restrictive descriptions notwithstanding, disnarration remains an open-ended feature in many ways. It may not always be easy in detective fiction to demarcate the false from the real solution. Sometimes a projected solution speculated upon by the fictional detective, which ultimately turns out to be false, may be required in the plot in order to be eliminated for the real solution to be revealed. Specifically, I am thinking of a novel like Barry Unsworth's *Morality Play*, which captures a historical moment in the evolution of English drama, in the transition made by a travelling troupe of players from playing abstract personifications to 'real' characters. Recognising an opportunity for their trade in the murder of a young boy in a town they pass through, they decide to play 'the murder of Thomas Wells'. Their performances are essentially reconstructions of the crime, which painstakingly, and through trial and error, lead

them to the truth of who really killed Wells. By the end of the novel, the young woman who had been arrested for the crime is revealed to have been innocent, because of the discovery of the true solution by the players *through* two false solutions which they subsequently revise. Would this false solution therefore, still be construed as the disnarrated portion of the text? Where does one draw the line? Prince surely recognizes the importance of this question when he points out that '[T]he disnarrated provides one of the important means for emphasizing tellability: this narrative is worth narrating because *it* could have been otherwise, because *it* usually is otherwise, because *it* was *not* otherwise' (5).

3. In my Introduction to this volume, I have attempted to describe the 'working' of disnarration in texts by reading a few well-known literary examples.
4. Prince quotes Labov who says: 'Pointless stories are met (in English) with the withering rejoinder, "So what?"Every good narrator is continually warding off this question' (5). The disnarrated addresses if implicitly, this question, by suggesting what could have happened.
5. A fact of which Fowles' narrator is aware when he declares that 'whichever is the second will seem, so strong is the tyranny of the last chapter, the final, the "real" version' (390).
6. Not just postmodern fiction, but also film. Robyn Warhol in 'Neonarrative' situates disnarration in *Run Lola Run* in its refusal to rest with the first two violent endings, by providing a third and happy ending as the conclusive one (thereby making disnarration a discourse-oriented feature rather than a part of the story) (229–31). This is underscored in the beginning of each of Lola's three sprints. Just after her mother asks her to buy shampoo, the film cuts to a television screen inside which we watch a cartoon version of Lola running down the stairs, before cutting back to the actor playing Lola. The insertion of a dimension through the television frame contributes to the self-reflexivity inherent in the three competing endings that the film provides. I am obliged to Nisha Viswanathan for drawing attention to the story-lives of the random people that Lola meets while running, whether the lady with the buggy or the lady in the bank corridor. The lives of these people stretched out into the future are laid out for the viewer as a series of successive snapshots. Their stories are never incorporated into the main story of Lola's run, and provide a text-book instance of disnarration.

7. This very detail from the plot of Austen's novel is used by Robyn Warhol in the opening paragraph of her comparative study of *Northanger Abbey* and *The Spoils of Poynton* in 'Narrative Refusals and Generic Transformation in Austen and James: What Doesn't Happen in *Northanger Abbey* and *The Spoils of Poynton*'.
8. But this is by no means an exhaustive definition, as not all resemblances qualify as *mise en abymes*. A *mise en abyme* typically posits two levels of discourse, one embedded within the other, with the latter reflecting the former thematically or structurally.
9. This is strengthened over the course of the narrative by the fact that the listeners comprising the imaginary children are not allowed to be forgotten by the reader; a narration of their responses periodically keeps interrupting the narrator's account in such sentences as '[H]ere Alice put out one of her dear mother's looks, too tender to be called upbraiding', or 'Here John tried to expand all his eyebrows and tried to look courageous'.

WORKS CITED

Austen, Jane. *Northanger Abbey*. 1818. New York: Random House, 2002. Print.

Fowles, John. *The French Lieutenant's Woman*. 1969. London: Vintage, 1996. Print.

Karttunen, Laura. 'A Sociolinguistic Perspective on Negatives and the Disnarrated: Lahiri, Roy, Rushdie.' *Partial Answers: Journal of Literature and the History of Ideas*. 6.2 (June 2008). 419–41.

Lamb, Charles. 'Dream-Children: A Revery.' Brander Matthews, ed. *The Short Story: Specimen Illustrating Its Development*. New York: American Book Company, 1907; Bartleby.com, 2000. www.bartleby.com/195/14 Dec. 2015.

Nelles, William. '*MISE EN ABYME*.' *Routledge Encyclopedia of Narrative Theory*. Eds. David Herman, Manfred Jahn and Marie-Laure Ryan. London and New York: Routledge, 2005, 2008. 312–13. Print.

Prince, Gerald. 'The Disnarrated.' *Style*. 22.1 (Spring 1988): 1–8.

Radcliffe, Ann. *A Sicilian Romance: A Gothic Novel.* 1790. Timeless Classic Books, 2010. Print.

———. *The Mysteries of Udolpho: A Gothic Romance.* 1794. Reader's Edition. Sacramento: Idle Spider Books, 2010. Print.

Run Lola Run. Dir. Tom Tykwer. 1998. Film. 29 May 2014. http://www.youtube.com/watch?v=1tIuD5aqc40

Ryan, Maurie-Laure. *Possible Worlds, Artificial Intelligence, and Narrative Theory.* Bloomington: Indiana UP, 1991. Print.

Unsworth, Barry. *Morality Play.* W.W.Norton and Co., 1996. Print.

Warhol, Robyn R. 'Narrative Refusals and Generic Transformation in Austen and James: What Doesn't Happen in *Northanger Abbey* and *The Spoils of Poynton.*' *The Henry James Review.* The Johns Hopkins UP, 28 (2007): 259–68. *Project Muse.* Web. 29 May 2014.

———. 'Neonarrative; or, How to Render the Unnarratable in Realist Fiction and Contemporary Film.' In *A Companion to Narrative Theory*, eds. James Phelan and Peter J. Rabinowitz. Oxford: Blackwell Publishing, 2005. 220–31. Print.

Section 1

Preview

The Rhetoric of Choice

Supriya Chaudhuri

'Shall I kill myself or have a cup of coffee?' Popular belief attributes this question to Albert Camus, but there is no proof that he ever actually said or wrote any such thing. Nevertheless, philosophers as reputable as Renata Salecl have credited Camus with thus posing the typically absurd dilemma of modern man, 'that one's very existence is always a matter of choice' ('Choice and the Ultimate Incurable', 87). I was reminded of this piece of Camus apocrypha in the bleakly futuristic setting of Delhi's Terminal 1: an airport specially designed for illiterates since it did not (at the time) have a bookshop. It was in these circumstances, surrounded by blandishments to shop, drink (one could buy a bottle of wine, though not a book), surf the Internet, have a full body massage, visit a spa, eat, pray, and sleep, that it struck me that most of these options were in fact foreclosed, since I had a flight to catch at a specific time. It seemed to me that the airport lounge, and my own situation, that of a traveller on a winter's night, was peculiarly representative of the postmodern condition. Postmodernity is itself heavily invested in a rhetoric of choice, appearing to open up, even to actively pursue, a surfeit of narrative options. This freedom is obviously linked to the cultural logic of late capital, as Fredric Jameson called it, and may seem to present the reverse of that denial of possibility that Gerald Prince described as disnarration, or rather, 'the disnarrated'. I would like to use the space of this paper to reflect on this apparent contrast, between narrative plurality and narrative foreclosure, and ask whether the two are as dissimilar as they appear.

Prince himself, in the celebrated article that set out very frugally the terms of his proposition, insisted on a distinction between the unnarratable (acts that fall below the threshold of narration, like the motions involved in breathing or walking), the unnarrated (events that are silently excluded from the fictional work) and the disnarrated, a narrative possibility that is specifically evoked only to be denied (Prince 1–8). For this he also suggested the French term *denarré,* which might have yielded the English *denarrated,* a past participle carrying a more negative implication than 'disnarrated'. In effect, though Prince does not say so, this is related to the rhetorical figure of *apophasis* (to mention something by not mentioning it) with its special variant *paraleipsis*, much used by Cicero and the classical rhetoricians to denigrate opponents: as in the statement 'I could enumerate here the many cruelties of Nero, but I will desist.' A similar but separate device, also linked in some ways to disnarration, is *aposiopesis*, where the sentence is deliberately broken off half-way and left trailing, its conclusion suspended. In classical rhetoric these devices deliberately invoke the missing information, even if the form of the utterance is negative or abortive: that is, the point is made by its elision. In rhetoric, this is a figure – paradoxically – of inclusion.

I find it interesting, then, that for Prince as for later commentators, the figure of the disnarrated in fiction suggests a rhetorical or ideological *exclusion*. The fact that something is mentioned is obviously an invitation to speculate on a narrative possibility: but the possibility is read under the sign of negation, of loss or silence. Perhaps Prince's reading, given his own scholarly location in French fiction, was decisively informed by the greatest example of a novel where the disnarrated becomes, as it were, the mode of being inhabited by the protagonist: Gustave Flaubert's *Madame Bovary*. Which of us could forget the following account of Emma's boredom: 'She gave up playing the piano. What use, with no one to hear her? Since she could never play at a concert, in a short-sleeved velvet gown, lightly caressing the keys of an Erard and feeling the murmurs of ecstasy wafting all about her like a breeze – it wasn't worth the boredom of practising' (Flaubert 76). Emma's reading of romantic novels, her memory of the lords and ladies at the ball, her yearning for a grand passion, for glamour and refinement, makes her the site of *narrative* expectations that can never be fulfilled, so that to her 'the future was an unlighted corridor with a stoutly locked door at the end of it' (76). What Flaubert conveys, with a masterly economy of means, is not only the impossibility of Emma's ever achieving the life of passion and excitement she craves, but the fact that in the banality of her everyday existence, she gives up what might otherwise have occupied her. 'What was the use? What was the use? Sewing got on her nerves' (76). For 'she remembered all her luxurious instincts, all the privations of her soul, the squalors of married life and housekeeping, her dreams dropping in the mud like wounded swallows, the things she had wanted and denied herself, the things she might have had!' (197). It is Emma Bovary, surely, a heroine who desires contrary impossibilities ('[s]he wanted to die, and she wanted to live in Paris' [73]), who is the most representative vehicle for the disnarrated in fiction. And Prince's choice of term might also have been influenced by his reading of the French *nouveau roman* as a fiction above all of disappointment, or, to use the accepted term, *déception*.

Disappointment, the blocking or thwarting of narrative possibility, is a crucial element of the modernist aesthetic. If *Madame Bovary* – or, say, *Anna Karenina* – powerfully evokes the absent state as present to desire and imagination, thus including by excluding like the classical rhetorical figure of *paraleipsis,* modernist fiction is much more ruthless in its treatment of an unrealized alternative. Take, for example, the adolescent hero of Alan Sillitoe's 'The Loneliness of the Long-Distance Runner', a Borstal boy who deliberately loses a race he could have won, in order to disappoint – in the most literal terms – the expectations of the institution's Governor. On the face of it this is a rather over-determined example of the disnarrated, since it is not inevitably but by choice that a narrative possibility is denied (Sillitoe 7–54). Nevertheless, modernist ideology itself is deeply invested in this negative imperative, so that the disnarrated repeatedly appears in modernist fiction not so much as an enabling possibility, but as a sign of defeat and hermeneutic loss, brilliantly captured at the close of Camus' *The Stranger*:

> Nothing, nothing mattered, and I knew why. So did he. Throughout the whole absurd life I'd lived, a dark wind had been rising toward me from somewhere deep into my future, across years that were still to come, and as it passed, this wind leveled whatever was offered to me at the time, in years no more real than the ones I was living. What did other people's deaths or a mother's love matter to me; what did his God or the lives people choose or the fate they think they elect matter to me when we're

> all elected by the same fate, me and billions of privileged people like him who also called themselves my brothers? (121)

Meursault's recognition of the inevitable foreclosing of narrative options in death opens him at last to 'the gentle indifference of the world' (122).

Modernist narrative invests in the disnarrated as a means of foreclosure, indicating the impossibility of human lives being other than they are; that is, as determined by the absurdity of reason's conflict with material circumstance. It would be wrong to say that human beings have no choice, but it is certainly the case that a single realised option negates everything else that could have happened but did not. As in Sillitoe's novel, one might claim this as a modernist ethic of sport (it is Camus, after all, who is, again apocryphally, credited with the statement 'All that I know most certainly about morality and obligations I owe to football.')[1]. But this gritty pessimism has subsequently yielded place to a postmodernist world of simulacra, of images projected as hyper-real substitutions for anything that might be conceived as *the game itself*. Typical of these amusements is Twenty20 cricket, with its endless looping of exactly similar matches played between exactly balanced international teams, all options open at all times. Cast into a surreal arena of performance where intense, speeded up recitals of skill can only be judged by the aesthetics of astonishment, with feats achieved only to be immediately surpassed (so that everyone is famous for thirty seconds, to misquote Andy Warhol), it is a form that combines hypnotic appeal with instant obsolescence, the condition of popular culture in a world of information technology. In fact one could say that T20 cricket is a parody of postmodern art forms, a populist takeover of the state of limitless repetition. And in fiction too, the disnarrated, with its sombre dystopic implications, has been suspended or replaced by an opening out of narrative possibility in the postmodernist rhetoric of choice.

Choice is a subject of interest to postmodern philosophers and sociologists like Renata Salecl, who cites both Althusser and Lacan to analyse the tyranny of choice under post-industrial capitalism (*Choice*, 9, 121–26).

In effect, the ideology of choice offers an illusion of subjective freedom, but the interpellated subject emerges as remarkably unfree, and the fetish-choices of the market impose new kinds of enslavement and anxiety. Without transferring this model in its entirety to postmodern fiction, it is worth noting that literature too can play with the notion of a limitless universe of alternatives. Let us take a well-known example of such a play, Italo Calvino's *If on a Winter's Night a Traveler*, first published in 1979. But Calvino began as a modernist during the great period of Italian neo-realist cinema with *The Path to the Spiders' Nests*, published more than thirty years earlier (1947) and all his subsequent writing is possessed by a never-to-be-fulfilled desire for the apparent truth and substantiality of the 'world' of realist fiction. In a preface that he composed for the third edition of that first book in 1964, he wrote revealingly of his own early ambitions as a neorealist: 'We were all content-driven, but there were never such obsessive formalists as us; we claimed to be a school of objective writers, but there were never such effusive lyricists as us' (*The Path to the Spiders' Nests*, 9). For the writers of the period, the world and its objects 'were simply there, so solid and indisputable that they seemed to us to be completely natural; for us the problem appeared to be one of poetics, of how to transform that world which for us was the world into a work of literature' (9–10).

Yet in the language of this ambiguous, self-critical Preface, Calvino is already anticipating a later phase that puts the object-world beyond reach: converts it, in effect, into a choice of fictions. Twenty years on from his first book, the author knows himself to inhabit a market where novels are 'the surplus goods of a society which is all too easily satisfied' (26). *If on a Winter's Night* presents itself to us in a bookshop:

> In the shop window you have promptly identified the cover with the title you were looking for. Following this visual trail, you have forced your way through the shop past the thick barricade of Books You Haven't Read, which were frowning at you from the tables and shelves, trying to cow you. But you know you must never allow yourself to be awed, that among them there extend for acres and acres the Books You Needn't Read, the

> Books Made For Purposes Other Than Reading, Books . . . . can be established. (10–11)

If on a Winter's Night offers a solution to this problem of choice, but while it appears to give us everything we might possibly want to read, it makes the act of reading impossibly self-conscious and unfree. How, we ask ourselves, can we wriggle out of the armchair officiously chosen for us by the writer, the posture he recommends with such impudent concern for our comfort? How are we to have thoughts he has not always/already anticipated? How, that is to say, can we avoid being his Implied Reader and retain a measure of opaqueness before his searching authorial gaze? For he has anticipated even this desire, and in Chapter Seven, he asks,

> What are you like, Other Reader? It is time for this book in the second person to address itself no longer to a general male you, perhaps brother and double of a hypocrite I, but directly to you who appeared already in the second chapter as the Third Person necessary for the novel to be a novel, for something to happen between the male Second Person and the female Third, for something to take form, develop, or deteriorate according to the phases of human events. (113)

This Other Reader, however distinct from the *hypocrite lecteur,* is nevertheless already glimpsed in the mirror of self. And if the tyrannical modernist *auteur* has been dissolved into no more than an effect of prose, he has been replaced by what seems very much like a compulsive postmodernist gamer, uncannily able to anticipate our responses. *If on a Winter's Night* is composed as a kind of literary treasure hunt, with a framing narrative involving two persons, two Readers (or more, depending on how you look at the mirrors) involved in a search for books that repeatedly disappear or transform themselves into other books, while they also seem to be caught up in international conspiracies, publishing rackets, romances, political plots, conflicts of genres: eventually it seems that like the good protagonists of the 19th century realist novel, they might get married. At the same time the book offers us ten sample chapters of the books these Readers set out to read, written as loose imitations of the content, if not precisely the style, of contemporary fictions as far apart as the spaghetti western and Yukio Mishima. What undercuts the imitation, however, is the knowledge that none of these novels can be finished: to some extent they all belong to that Cimmerian space of splendid, acrobatic literary feats in a 'dead' language, or one whose death has been prematurely announced. As Calvino says, and here he sounds uncommonly like Milan Kundera: 'my working method has more often than not involved the subtraction of weight. I have tried to remove weight, sometimes from people, sometimes from heavenly bodies, sometimes from cities; above all I have tried to remove weight from the structure of stories and from language' (*Six Memos for the Next Millennium*, 3).

Through the ten chapters of his ten books, as in the frame-narrative itself, Calvino is looking back at the enthralling, but (for him) always-already doomed enterprise of the novel, the provision of an alternative reality. His own enterprise is to rob that reality of weight, of substance, by showing us how phantasmal, how constructed, how readily interrupted (for example by the loss of the rest of the book) it always was. In the last of the story-sections, 'What story down there awaits its end?' Calvino returns to the foundations of the European novel:

> Walking along the great Prospect of our city, I mentally erase the elements I have decided not to take into consideration. I pass a ministry building, whose facade is laden with caryatids, columns, balustrades, plinths, brackets, metopes; and I feel the need to reduce it to a smooth vertical surface, a slab of opaque glass, a partition that defines space without imposing itself on one's sight. But even simplified like this, the building still oppresses me: I decide to do away with it completely: in its place a milky sky rises over the bare ground. . . . In the bustle of the Prospect I keep meeting people the sight of whom, for various reasons, is unpleasant to me: my superiors, because they remind me of my inferior position; my inferiors, because I hate to feel possessed of an authority I consider petty, as petty as the envy, servility and bitterness it inspires. I erase both categories, without any hesitation: out of the corner of my eye, I see them shrink and vanish in a faint wisp of fog. (*If on a Winter's Night*,193)

What Calvino's narrator erases here is surely Gogol's Nevsky Prospekt, turning the fictional world that had crept out of Gogol's overcoat (as Dostoyevsky described it) into no more than a wisp of fog, a regulated space that will accommodate only the object of desire: in this case the imaginary beloved, Franziska. Too late, he realises that he has made a mistake; he wants to bring the world back again, closing and reopening his eyes in the desperate hope that the Prospect, teeming with traffic and light and noise, will surround him once more – but 'the void all around us is more and more void' (*If on a Winter's Night*, 197). What he has once got rid of will never return to him in its former fullness and immediacy, and what the future holds, as the men from Section D tell him, is uncertain. That future is the future of postmodernist fiction, which has abolished the world or reduced it to alternative stylistic possibilities. Here, too, Franziska beckons, 'her small face a bit chapped from the cold', inviting the narrator to a meeting in a cafe lined with mirrors, but an abyss lies between her and his desire (198–99).

Was it necessary, we may ask, to shatter all our illusions so completely? For despite the undercutting of every section as it is composed, each casts its spell. There is considerable power in the modernist bleakness of 'leaning from the steep slope', its anxious, paranoid obsession with signs and symbols. Yet just as we feel attuned to its neurotic narrator and Miss Zwida, 'an irreparable rent' is opened up in the perfect order of its language. That language is Cimmerian: that is, it is a dead language, incorporating into its very being the supreme deathliness of modernism, its reduction of the living world into the frozen, spectral landscape of allegory (as Walter Benjamin described it in *The Origin of German Tragic Drama*, 166). And this rupture, this breach, takes place over and over again; in some of the sample chapters, what we get is not an imitation or parody of a particular fictional style, but a tissue of echoes and allusions always-already undermined by the narrator's insistent awareness of its facticity. Thus, in 'In a network of lines that intersect', the narrator says:

> It is my image that I want to multiply, but not out of narcissism or megalomania, as could all too easily be believed: on the contrary, I want to conceal, in the midst of so many illusory ghosts of myself, the true me, who makes them move. . . . . These pages I am writing should also transmit a cold luminosity, as in a mirrored tube, where a finite number of figures are broken up

> and turned upside down and multiplied. If my figure sets out in all directions and is doubled at every corner, it is to discourage those who want to pursue me. (129)

So is this apparition of choice, the multiplicity of narrative options realised and presented in the magical liaisons of Calvino's prose, an answer to the bleakness of modernist disnarration? I would suggest that it isn't: that choice itself is an illusion in a market where our ability to buy is strictly limited by the poverty of our own being. The *disnarrated*, a category that to Prince is expressive of the constraints of narrative coherence as such, inhabits Calvino's fictions as a collection of dead bodies come to life. These bodies are not just spectral in themselves, they render everything they touch unreal by association. (As Hobbes says of Calvin's snowmen, 'I note that your oeuvre is monochromatic.') (Watterson). What is produced is not a contrast of narration and disnarration, but *narration as disnarration,* as though postmodernism had not recovered from modernism's loss of faith in history and in time. If time is a succession of present instants, and history a construction, variable through its telling, persons, objects and places can no longer claim that investment of faith and love that the realist text demands. The world of postmodernist fiction is either posited as a site of free imaginative play, of making and unmaking, or of commodity fetishism where objects acquire a hyperreal distinctiveness and iconicity, but fail to convince us that they actually exist (as in advertising, the pre-eminent postmodernist art-form).

Commodity fetishism might provide a point of entry into the work of the contemporary Japanese novelist Haruki Murakami, a writer whose work produces a species of postmodern addiction. Yet why should these stories of contemporary Tokyo, with their unattached, job-shy young male protagonists, eating spaghetti and pizza, knowledgeable about Western music and European fiction, chasing lost cats, descending into wells, noting the finer points of women's earlobes and their feet, having telephone conversations, listening to stories, draw us into their spaces and times? As fictions, they seem curiously detached from Japanese culture and literary tradition, and they do not require us to relate them to the great Japanese modernists we have all read in translation, such as Yukio Mishima, Kenzaburo Oe, or Yasunari Kawabata. Modern Japanese literature (beginning after the Meiji restoration in 1868) drew upon European traditions, but it was with Murakami that the American style became 'cool' and fashionable, and his protagonists inhabit a cultural space apparently indistinguishable from metropolitan 'American' existence worldwide; they run and go to the gym, they wear casual clothes like T-shirts and shorts, they eat non-Japanese global food, they listen to classical music or jazz, they read Western literature. Despite the fact that the books are set in Japan and are wholly contemporary, indeed autobiographical, in tone (the student protagonist of *Norwegian Wood* is a lot like the young Haruki Murakami when he first came to Tokyo from Kobe), there are relatively few markers of a distinctively Japanese culture. Is this what urban existence in post-60s Japan is like, or has Murakami chosen to dispense with indigenous markers of authenticity to market a global 'coolness' and urbanity, a youth culture, that can take its place anywhere? Murakami's internationalism guarantees that his novels sell far more in translation than in the original Japanese.

It is at this point that we need to reflect on the coincidence, so marked in Murakami, of postmodernism with postmodernity, that is, of the style with the substance of late capitalist culture. Murakami's critics accuse him of writing American novels in Japanese, of acting as entrepreneur of a globalised material culture in a world of merchandise and commodity fetishism, and of employing a style that, despite its invocation of the surreal, abolishes depth and substitutes a surface play of signs. The very aesthetic of his work provides a report on postmodern knowledge, of the 'cultural logic of late capital', to use Jameson's phrase (Jameson, n.p.). Murakami reflects the abstract Americanisation of contemporary culture, the 'irresistible and irreversible globalization of economic and cultural exchanges' as Michael Hardt and Antonio Negri put it in their analysis of a postcolonial *Empire* (xi). This is capable even of colonising the subconscious, as in Murakami's surreal *Hard-Boiled Wonderland* (1985), and necessarily affects the way reality is represented. Murakami's irony, the fissures that run through his narrative and bifurcate it into alternative life-worlds, the incursion of the surreal or the magical into ordinary existence, render metonymy, the primary instrument of realism, ineffective. The pleasant anonymity of his characters' lives is at the same time a condition of hollowness or extreme, even suicidal, despair. His abstract 'Americanness' must be set against his repeated invocation of Kafka, (as in *Kafka on the Shore*), indicating a representational paradox at the heart of his fiction, which seeks to treat surface as depth, in the style of modernist allegory, but only succeeds in making a generic substitution, of fantasy for fable.

Murakami deliberately refuses conformity with Japanese *jun-bungaku* (pure literature, or high art) by choosing to align his work with popular forms: pop music, thrillers, sci-fi, romances, mysteries, bestsellers. This too is a postmodern trick, annulling the differences between high and low art, apparently to democratise both content and form, but in the interests of a more radical anarchy. Murakami's characters are marked by aimlessness and anomie, rejecting the world's apparent fullness and purpose; they are skilled in small tasks but devoid of larger ambitions; his protagonists are often unemployed young men, drawn to beautiful, mysterious, whimsical, suicidal women. This is not to say that Murakami is incapable of engaging with history, as he does for example in *The Wind-up Bird Chronicle*. Yet the real *habitus* of his characters is a kind of style or mode of existence, not primarily a place.

The *Wind-up Bird Chronicle* is an intensely 'connected' novel, working out an intricate thread of relatedness between all the characters who pass through its pages. At the same time, it plays with our contemporary experiences of disjunction, so that the narrator can scarcely predict whether he will find the cat, meet the telephone woman, discover that his wife has a lover, or spend time at the bottom of a well. At any given time, he has 'no more plans for the afternoon than a migrating bird has collateral assets' (82) and as the novel proceeds, he feels

> a strange detachment, as if I were trying to leap from one moving vehicle to another that was moving at a different speed. I existed in the empty space between the two, a vacant house.

> I was now a vacant house, just as the Miyawaki house had once been. This woman had come into the vacant house and, for some unknown reason, was running her hands all over the walls and pillars. Whatever her reason might be, vacant house that I was (and I was that and nothing more) I could do nothing (I needed to do nothing) about it. (368)

The narrator is both everything and nothing. 'I struggled to superimpose my own image upon that of a vacant house. I thought of myself as a pillar, a wall, a ceiling, a floor, a roof, a window, a door, a stone. It seemed the most reasonable thing to do. . . Separating from the flesh is not so difficult. It can put me far more at ease, allow me to cast off the discomfort I feel. I am a weed-choked garden, a flightless stone bird, a dry well' (368).

We should note the present tense here: the narrator is what he feels himself to be. But he is not any of these things in the same way as Kafka's Gregor Samsa is a large insect – that is, irreversibly. Narrative possibilities, sequentially pursued and abandoned in Murakami's fiction, are signs rather than routes. And the efficacy of signs is undone by hermeneutic excess, so that we do not in the end know what they mean. The wind-up bird appears in the first chapter, linked to the missing cat ('Noboru Wataya/ Where are you?/Did the wind-up bird/ Forget to wind your spring?' 23), and eventually it becomes an agent that keeps the world in motion, linked to Toru Okada, who is called 'Mr Wind-up Bird' by May and imagines himself as the wind-up bird when he is in the well (256). He hears Schumann's piano piece called 'Bird as Prophet' (278); his ornithologist uncle has never heard of such a bird (288); Creta Kano is like the prophet bird that lived in the forest (313); the bird is heard calling during the zoo massacre (403), but Nutmeg Akasaka cannot remember it (404); the vet did not hear it (409); Toru is like the bird-catcher in *The Magic Flute* (406); Toru reads Cinnamon's 'Wind-up Bird Chronicle', with its mention of the bird's cry that no one could hear any longer (522); 'the cry of this bird was audible only to certain special people' (525); the waiter whistles *The Thieving Magpie* (554), just as the narrator was doing at the start (5). Yet, at the end of the novel, we do not hear the bird's call, only the sound of a woodpecker. How can we interpret a symbol so richly burdened? As with so much else in Murakami, there is here a curious simultaneity of poetic immediacy and metaphysical delay, of presence and absence, plenitude and lack. Magical, even mesmerising in its charm, Murakami's world draws us into the paradoxes of postmodernist aesthetics. It offers us meanings like spells or gifts, but it also signals the failure of meaning in ordinary lives and ordinary hopes. In consequence, it renders the category of the *disnarrated* redundant, since we are never sure what is included or excluded in a fictional universe where everything is possible but nothing is realised.

This is not simply a *reductio ad absurdum* of the promise of plenitude which the postmodern text makes but cannot sustain. The category of the *disnarrated,* in classic realist and modernist texts, is located in a certain experience of time. It appears as a way of encoding narrative possibilities that have what Yuri Lotman would call a minus function (51). Importantly, these possibilities are metonymically, rather than metaphorically, linked to the action: they are contiguous with the plot, like limbs that are cut off, doors that are closed. To engage with, to redeem or abolish, the category of the disnarrated, postmodern fiction has to redeem or abolish modernity's understanding of time. This cannot be done simply by opening up an infinitude of possibilities – by employing, that is to say, a rhetoric of choice.

Almost at the end of the greatest of all postmodern novels, Gabriel Garcia Marquez's *A Hundred Years of Solitude,* the arthritic priest says to Aureliano Buendia, 'My son, it is enough to be sure that you and I exist at this moment' (376). Aureliano, appalled by the weight of history ('he was unable to bear in his soul the crushing weight of so much past') and seeing 'the epigraph of the parchments perfectly placed in the order of man's time and space: *The first of the line is tied to a tree and the last is being eaten by the ants*' (381), retreats before it. He nails up the doors and windows of his house and devotes himself to deciphering the history of his family written by Melquiades in Sanskrit, 'which was his mother tongue', and in this history Melquiades 'had not put events in the order of man's conventional time, but had concentrated a century of daily episodes in such a way that they coexisted in one instant' (382). As Aureliano reads, skipping ahead because he is already familiar with some of the details, the wind begins to blow, and the more he reads, and skips, and notes the predictions and repetitions, and arrives at the instant that he is living, prophecy and experience come together, and the wind becomes a 'fearful whirlwind of dust and rubble being spun about by the wrath of the biblical hurricane' (382–83). He understands not only that he is to die, but that 'the city of mirrors (or mirages) would be wiped out by the wind and exiled from the memory of men at the precise moment when Aureliano Babilonia would finish deciphering the parchments' (383).

This wind is the storm that Walter Benjamin describes in his 'Theses on the Philosophy of History': blowing from Paradise and piling up the debris at the feet of the Angel whose face is turned towards the past, but whose wings are spread to the storm (Benjamin 259–60). But if there are two kinds of time in Benjamin, the homogeneous empty time of history (266) and the *jetztzeit* or time of the now, there are three kinds of time in Marquez's novel. The history of Macondo is a sequential progression in linear time, and at any moment we can plot where we are in the linear scale through memory or prophecy. 'Many years later, as he faced the firing squad, Colonel Aureliano Buendia was to remember that distant afternoon when his father took him to discover ice' (7). At the time of its first settlement Macondo is new, like Eden: no one has yet died in it, and many things do not have names, so that one has to indicate them by pointing. There follow inventions, discoveries, wars, oppression, atrocities, migrations, returns, and finally decay and destruction. The genealogical line of the Buendia family is precisely drawn, and its members enact, over a hundred years, an unrepeatable sequence of events. The inexorable progression of this linear timescale (time as arrow) is what Aureliano Babilonia feels as the 'crushing weight of so much past': despite its relative isolation, its lack of importance in the scale of world history or European time, Macondo is not a *space taken out of time*. It is time-bound, not timeless. But there is also in the experience of events in Macondo a sense of the cyclic nature of time (time as wheel) sometimes linked to mythic time, or the myth of eternal return. The novel's plot makes this an aspect of family history, a version of phylogeny repeating ontogeny, emphasised by the repetition of names. In the Buendia family the Jose Arcadios are practical and combative, the Aurelianos philosophical and withdrawn; women called Ursula are strong and nurturing, women called Remedios are beautiful and die young – and so on. By repeating the sexual adventures, the mistakes and hopes of their ancestors, the members of the Buendia family produce a narrative history that reads like a mythic cycle of repetition.

Ostensibly, such a structure offers humanity both more hope and more despair: instead of being pushed forward unceasingly on the path of time's arrow towards an unknown future (Benjamin's 'homogeneous empty time' citation), we can hope for time's wheel to bring us back again to the beginning – though we may also fear being trapped in this endless repetition of history as myth. While the structure of *One Hundred Years* gives us a powerful sense of cyclic time, at the end Marquez seems to cancel it out, by telling us that Macondo's history can never be repeated, because 'races condemned to one hundred years of solitude did not have a second opportunity on earth' (383). But there is a third time, as viewed in Melquiades' Sanskrit parchments, where a century of daily events appear to coexist in one instant, where time and experience are viewed *sub specie aeternitas*. When Aureliano Babilonia understands his life and his history in this way, he precipitates his own extinction, because he and all his family are but a speck in that wind that blows from eternity. Aureliano's reading the parchments is also a figure for our reading of Marquez's book: the book is where a century of daily events are brought together in a brief space, a space which closes forever with the closing of the book.

These three views of time are simultaneously present in the book: that is, we are not asked to choose between them, though it is the first that dominates. The idea of time as inexorable progression is after all the controlling illusion of our human lives – it is difficult to think 'logically' in terms of time as dimension, to rationalise, in commonsense terms, the quantum universe, since ordinary logic is also temporal. In that respect human thought is trapped in time's flow. Allegorically, the history of Macondo is the history of Latin America, as Marquez implies in his Nobel lecture; the novel suggests this through a persistent (sometimes tedious) use of allegorical detail, such as the colour of the Buendia house. Because of its late beginning and relative isolation, Macondo experiences modernity as a series of upheavals or discoveries. This is characteristic, we may note, of colonised cultures, where there is a sudden, sometimes catastrophic encounter between conflicting knowledge-systems (as with the advent of clock-time, the railways and the telegraph.) The gipsies bring marvellous new knowledge or implements to Jose Arcadio Buendia, and he repeats, with his limited resources, the great discoveries or inventions of European science, though to no purpose. Politics, government, war, are also experienced in this way: as external intrusions which then take hold of the people of Macondo and cause their suffering.

The lag, or lack, that separates the history of Macondo from the history of the European world has two consequences. Firstly, it removes the distinction between magical, mythic time and real time; and secondly, it hollows out Macondo's history by robbing it of its significance in universal history. The science and progress of Europe (as communicated by the gipsies) seem just as magical and improbable as levitation by means of chocolate (performed by Father Nicanor, 82). The fruitless wars waged by Colonel Aureliano Buendia, the massacre of the banana workers, have virtually no impact on the 'world' outside. Macondo experiences its own history as inexorable sequence, but that history is a repetition – both tragic and farcical – of universal history, and it is also full of repetitions and echoes within itself. At the end of the novel we are left with the relentless assault of the red ants, and the wind that will blow Macondo to dust. Macondo has undergone, we may say, a speeded-up version of universal history, and now it is close to its end.

Seen as the text contained in Melquiades' parchments, Macondo's history is eternally present, contained in the instant that it is viewed and understood. This is the time of the book, the time of the text. To read and understand oneself is to bring to a close the two other kinds of time: time as sequential chain and time as mythic cycle. The images Marquez uses in this last passage are strongly apocalyptic, and there is even a reference to the Biblical hurricane. The apocalypse or end of the world, as described in the *Revelations* of St John, is of course a temporal event. In the Christian or Judaic schema it not only brings time's arrow to a conclusion, it provides 'the strait gate through which the Messiah might enter' as Benjamin puts it (264). The return of the Messiah confirms the embedding of time's arrow within time's cycle, the confining of linear time within cyclic time. In *Revelations* this moment is founded on a reading, the reading of a text which is also a prophecy. Yet Aureliano's end is the conclusion of a secular destiny: his life is lived in a time-scheme as irrevocable as that of Oedipus, but it is also the fulfilment of a prophecy. It ends at the precise moment when his substance and that of Macondo are grasped by us as text, understood as a function of the human word. In the end, *One Hundred Years of Solitude* is a novel about the novel – and modernity. It offers a postmodern understanding of narrative, but it rejects the rhetoric of choice, since it urges us to place our faith in the moment itself of reading.

Notes

1. 'Ce que finalement je sais de plus sûr sur la morale et les obligations des hommes, c'est au football que je le dois.' As quoted by Jean Noury in *Archives du Sénat français, Comptes rendus des débats*, Volume 4 (10 November 1965). Web. 13 October 2015. <http://www.senat.fr/comptes-rendus-eances/5eme/pdf/1965/11/s19651110_1551_1598.pdf>
   The Albert Camus Society states that the statement was made by Camus in a contribution to a university alumni magazine: see <http://www.camus-society.com/camus-football.html>

WORKS CITED

Benjamin, Walter. 'Theses on the Philosophy of History.' In *Illuminations*. Trans. Harry Zohn. Ed. Hannah Arendt. London: Fontana, 1977. Print.

———. *The Origin of German Tragic Drama*. Trans. John Osborne. London: New Left Books, 1977. Print.

Calvino, Italo. *If on a Winter's Night a Traveler*. Trans. William

Weaver. London: Picador, 1982. Print. Trans. of *Se una notte d'inverno un viaggiatore*, 1979.

———. *Six Memos for the Next Millennium*. Cambridge, Mass.: Harvard UP, 1988. Print.

———.*The Path to the Spiders' Nests*. Trans. Archibald Colquhoun and Martin McLaughlin. Rev. ed. New York: Ecco/ HarperCollins, 2000. Print. Trans. of *Il sentiero dei nidi di ragno*, 1947.

Camus, Albert. *The Stranger*. Trans. Matthew Ward. New York: Vintage, 1989. Print.

Flaubert, Gustave. *Madame Bovary: A Story of Provincial Life*. Trans. Alan Russell. Harmondsworth: Penguin Books, 1975. Print.

Hardt, Michael and Antonio Negri. 2000. *Empire*. Cambridge, Mass.: Harvard UP, 2003. Print.

Jameson, Fredric. *Postmodernism: or, The Cultural Logic of Late Capitalism*. Durham: Duke UP, 1992. Print.

Lotman, Yuri. *The Structure of the Artistic Text*. Trans. Ronald Vroom. Ann Arbor: Michigan Slavic Contributions VII, 1977. Print.

Marquez, Gabriel Garcia. *One Hundred Years of Solitude*. Trans. Gregory Rabassa. Harmondsworth: Penguin Books, 1975. Print.

Murakami, Haruki. *The Wind-up Bird Chronicle*. Trans. Jay Rubin. London: Vintage, 2003. Print.

Noury, Jean. *Archives du Sénat français, Comptes rendus des débats*. Volume 4 (10 November 1965). Web. 13 October 2015. <http://www.senat.fr/comptes-rendus-seances/5eme/pdf/1965/11/s19651110_1551_1598.pdf>

Prince, Gerald. 'The Disnarrated'. *Style* 22.1 (1988): 1–8. Print.

Salecl, Renata. 'Choice and the Ultimate Incurable', *Umbr(a): Incurable*, 1 (2006): 85–98. Print.

———.*Choice*. London: Profile Books, 2010. Print.

Sillitoe, Alan. 'The Loneliness of the Long-Distance Runner.' *The Loneliness of the Long-Distance Runner*. New York: Alfred A.Knopf, 1960. 7–54. Print.

Watterson, Bill. *'Calvin and Hobbes.'* 21 February 1990. Web. 2 February 2015. <http://www.gocomics.com/calvinandhobbes/1990/02/21>

Erasures, Silences and Recodings

The Writer in Search of Meaning

Jasbir Jain

'Mother died today. Or maybe yesterday; I can't be sure' (Camus 13). When Camus begins *The Outsider* with this opening statement, he confesses to the uncertainty of all knowledge and the shift in the time of the telling and its reception. Consequent on making the statement, he immediately dislocates it. Cyril Connolly, in his Introduction to the 1946 edition of the novel observed that, 'when we study its philosophy, the limpid style disguises a certain confusion' (8) and reflects the 'unreality of bourgeois ethic' (10). Disnarration is embedded not only in language through its various conditionals and connectives such as 'maybe', 'perhaps', 'but', 'nevertheless', 'if' and 'as well as', the prefixes and suffixes, but it is also embodied in the relationship of the human mind to the external world, the world of so-called reality, which is multi-layered and subject to different perceptions both by individuals and cultures. There is no way one can get away from the invisible link between ontology and epistemology, between ways of 'being' and of 'knowing'.

In the present paper, I propose first to develop on these connections between the external world and the writer's search for meaning in order to explore the multiple writerly struggles, and then proceed to analyse the significance of the processes and shifts for narratology by focusing on a couple of specific texts. The first task, strangely enough, sends us to the workings of an insane mind, which was an engagement with madness, a mind at odds with external reality. Foucault's work, *Madness and Civilisation* (1967), was to come much later and is related to the societal institutions of exclusion and confinement. Prior to that, in addition to the haunted characters of many a woman writer across cultures and histories, ranging from Bronte's Bertha Mason *(Jane Eyre)* to the heroine of Charlotte Perkin Gilman's' 'The Yellow Wallpaper', the subsequent discourses on this female malady

(Elaine Showalter) erroneously situated in gender, we also have male writers turning to this 'Other' as in Gogol's 'The Diary of a Madman' in the early 1830s.[1] Caught between the rationality of the Enlightenment and the irrational human responses, madness was the right answer to the situation where the madman is capable of finding 'completely logical (in his eyes) reasons for everything that happen to him' (Ronald Wilks' Introduction to the *Diary of a Madman and Other Stories,* 9). An underlying theme is the need to accommodate the anonymity of the growing urban world and its overpowering, rapid rush into modernity. In several ways, Gogol lays the ground for Kafka in this and in the story, 'The Overcoat', by stressing the repetitiveness of everyday occupations and the impersonal bureaucratic world.

In 'The Diary of a Madman', the madman's intentions are nearly always thwarted either through others or through inertia. And through failures and transcriptions, he wills his own appropriation of the place of King of Spain (35). There is a heading, 'No date the day didn't have one', a statement transferring a blankness to calendar time (37). There follows another, hardly twenty lines after this: 'I don't remember the date. There wasn't any month either. Damned if I know what it was'; indicating a disconnection with any identifiable moment, a lapse of memory and unreliability in narration. Another subheading follows a couple of pages later 'Da 34 te Mth eary 349' turning everything topsy-turvy, wishing for both salvation and annihilation at the same time and locked in a personal disconnected world (40–41).

Madness and the doppelganger are early examples of disnarration.[2] Omissions and silences are others. There is a similar preoccupation with madness in Dostoyevsky's work in a number of short stories, novellas and full-length work such as in *The Double, The Idiot, Notes from the Underground* and the story 'Bobok'. The feeling of being at odds with reality, the desire as well as the inability to alter perceived or sensed realities, the sense of being haunted or persecuted, the imperative to leave Russia because of its oppressive laws – this sense of crisis permeates the major nineteenth-century Russian texts and acts as mediator between reality and the intellectual perception of this reality. The metaphor often used is that of a madman or a split self. It can also be perceived in the Gothic as well as the mystery novel, which at one level worked through realistic narrative and at another travelled to the shared inner world of the writer and his character/s. The latter reflected the chaos that refused to make sense or be stated in direct terms.

The disappearance of a steady, reliable world and the gradual erosion of religious faith together disrupted phenomenological realities. Retrospectively, the connections between existentialism, absurdity and the rising totalitarian powers are more than obvious. One can sense it in the whole corpus of Kafka's work and later in the literature of the post-Second World War world in Gabriel Garcia Marquez and Milan Kundera, as they open out images of disconnected realities, free-floating identities, and question the meaning of life and death. We have some early examples of this disillusionment in the work of Arthur Koestler and George Orwell. The latter beautifully captured erasures, silences and recodings through the Ministry of Truth, Newspeak and Doublethink. Memory, both collective and individual; the narrative, whether historical or (a) personal (diary), are all rendered equally unreliable. Words change their meaning, the referential does not remain the same, and Winston's diary, like that of Gogol's madman, is located in a sense of uncertainty both of time and space.

Orwell, in *Nineteen Eighty-Four,* questions the validity of mere empiricism, and of an epistemology which derives its strength from phenomena. There are layers of tissues between the two; reality is never one-dimensional; it is not also embodied only in the individual response. The validation provided by the inward reflection is limited. Hence the need to speak, to write and to share – to communicate – but how do you get to that point when language itself is flawed, or controlled, or limited?

Confession plays an important role in *Nineteen Eighty-Four*. The confessional act, however, belies all truths. It is a fabricated response; in the long run this false self penetrates his inviolate self. Winston's obsession with two plus two adding to four is not only an echo from Dostoyevsky's *Notes from the Underground* (32) and the Russian writer Zamyatin's *We*, but also from the Kantian theory of knowledge. Kant categorises mathematical judgments as synthetic *a priori,* which, being universally valid, are independent of verification through experience (20–24). The sinister aspect of the game is that external reality can be controlled and as O' Brien tells Winston, the Party was capable of producing even a dual system of astronomy (213). Reversal, disnarration, altering or destroying the past and liquidating all moral values are part of this world. When certain conceptual possibilities can find no correspondence in the external world, they are reduced to becoming incommunicable. At one point Winston Smith wonders about the nature of existence: 'Did not the statement, "You do not exist", contain a logical absurdity?' (209). But it can easily be effected through torture. Winston's reality is controlled through words; the denial of his existence is a disnarration of his entity by destroying what Kant refers to as 'the subjective condition of sensibility under which alone outer intuition is possible for us' (71).

Why did the literature of silence and of non-communication come into being at a particular point in European literary history? Why did Beckett turn to monosyllable, unrelated dialogues, incomprehensible long monologues requiring connections and deciphering, as in *Waiting for Godot,* and to space and silence in his stage plays, *Play I* and *Play II*? Not in defiance of the textual preoccupation of New Criticism, not even as pure theatrical experiments, but as visual and verbal images of disnarration. The contemporary art movements – Surrealism, Dadaism, Cubism and a host of others – were, in themselves, attempts to draw attention to the incommunicable and the difficult but necessary conjunction of narration with disnarration. But the combination of mediums possible in painting and drama is not necessarily available to the writer who is wedged between his own apprehension of the world and the limits of language. Madness, confession, surrender and merger emerge as some possibilities. Some of these are realised in Franz Kafka's *The Trial* when K comes across not only the neutrality of the court, but also the impersonal attitude of the individual, as priests and chaplains withdraw and all past emotions are wiped out (*The Trial* 244) and realising this (247), gives himself unto death, despite the desire to go on.

Kafka's and Beckett's work call attention to the two different agencies involved in any act of communication: the speaker and the listener, the writer and the reader. Kafka was reluctant to publish, a reluctance which Max Brod locates in some of his unhappy experiences that 'drove him to a kind of self-sabotage' (252). Posthumously published, *The Trial* is an account of the multilayered reality when Franz and K are two divided beings, and there is a total absence of knowledge, of accountability enveloped in a total secrecy. The verbal communication is a complete miscarriage of communicability. Rights are wiped out, freedom is curtailed and his search for a proof of identity takes a long time. By the entry of the strangers in his room, all that he can understand and relate to is brushed away, and his papers declared irrelevant. There is no way he can get through this enclosure of non-being. Is this also a form of disnarration when known realities and procedures are brushed aside and he is advised to be reticent; a disnarration of the ordinary course of storytelling and empirical reality?

Disnarration takes place at another level when the writer, through external pressure, is compelled to re-narrate it. Gogol had to revise sections of *Dead Souls* in order to satisfy the censors (11). Interpreted in this larger context, very often a cultural narrative is engaged in disnarrating the mainstream structure. Toni Morrison in her essay, 'Unspeakable Things Unspoken: The Afro American Presence in Literature' (123–63) speaks of the silences and erasures imposed on the black presence. Morrison goes on to inquire, 'What intellectual feats had to be performed by the author or his critic to erase me from a society seething with my presence, and what effect has that performance had on the work? What are the strategies of escape from knowledge? Or of useful oblivion?' (136). And then, in her novels, proceeds to bring into her work the patterns of African speech and culture, the women's gossipy voices, the secrets shared, the uncertainty of being safe; in fact, the whole gamut of '[T]he subliminal, the underground life of a novel is the area most likely to link arms with the reader and facilitate making it one's own' (161).[3]

Steiner, in his essays in *Language and Silence,* has dwelt upon the 'retreat from the word' and the poet's silence. Linking it with the mid-twentieth century political atmosphere he comments on two things. One, the 'submission of successively larger areas of knowledge to the modes and proceeding of mathematics' (34) and two, that language has lost its connect with real (32). The word is disabled, 'language can only deal meaningfully with a special, restricted segment of reality. The rest, and it is presumably the larger part, is silence' (41).[4] Art has moved towards painting and music for exactly the reason that the world of the word has shrunk, and language has died in the 'face of the inhuman' ('Silence and the Poet', 73). Referring to Ionesco, he quotes from his Journal, '[T]here are no words for the deepest experience. The more I try to explain myself the less I understand myself' (qtd. 74). It is this inability to express the inhuman that leads the writer to write and erase, to cancel, to re-inscribe and to question.

Innumerable narratives get written, trying to state the inexpressible and cancel out earlier statements regarding morality, rationality, friendship, identity and community. It is in this context that Slavoj Zizek commented that 'in order to cope with a trauma, we symbolize' (qtd. by Julian Wolfreys 126), but this act of symbolisation can take many forms such as dreams, nightmares, phobias, and act through cancellations and denials.

The last two centuries have had a fair share of risings, revolutions and repressions. The European novel from Gogol onwards to writers such as Milan Kundera, is an attempt to live with these repressions and censorships, and resurrect the human entity. The question of the survival of literary art in times of terror – as the Indian poet Robin Ngangom has pointed out – is of utmost importance. How does the writer express the two: the turmoil in his mind, and the one outside? How does he survive? No longer does one refer to the holocaust victims as victims but as survivors.

But the survivors are not unscathed. There are memories and uncertainties and fears that stay with them, this 'unresolved experience', as observed by Ulrica Baer, who points out that there is a two-fold *structural* disjunction between an experience and its integration into narrative memory, understanding and communicability. Experiences of this kind may continue to exist in the psyche, but not necessarily surface in memory (Baer qtd. by Julian Wolfreys, 128–29).

The point I wish to make is that the nature of reality has a multiplicity; is ungraspable even if not totally incomprehensible, and hence the resort to disnarration, which enables a grasping of both narration and its cancellation. What happens to the sense of 'self', and how does one relate to the 'other' – the persecutor and the enemy? Does this kind of writing have any therapeutic value (for the survivor as well as the recorder) or does it require a different kind of reading, that goes beyond the mere act of reading to evoke an ethical response in us?

It is difficult to single out any of Kafka's writings as an illustrative example, mainly because all of them carry this sense of claustrophobia, powerlessness, incomprehension and dysfunction. Nevertheless, I have chosen two short stories as an illustration of the contradictory statements and the narration which fluctuates between two perspectives woven in statements, contradictions and oppositional reasoning, attempting to address questions of 'why' and 'how'. At the same time, there is an understanding of the human need for power and the equally human need to break free of that control.

'The Great Wall of China' represents the disrupted continuity of history. It also shows up the wrong-headed monophobic notion of nationalism, and exposes the myth of eternal power. The wall is used as a symbol of contemporary European politics, the relationship of self and the other, and the artificial demonising of the 'other': in this case, the Jew. There is no way to distinguish between the strong and the weak. The parabolic nature of the story is also more than evident. The Great Wall is built from two different locations, by different gangs of workers; no one has an overview, the two ends do not meet, and hence it fails to protect and has instead opened the doors to perpetual fear and uncertainty. The very intention of constructing the wall is undermined and undone.

Similarly in 'The Burrow' which, like the Great Wall, is also designed to be a place of protection, there are two burrows, one falsifies the description and is shallow, striking against natural firm rock. Another is camouflaged and covered by a movable layer of moss. In reality, it too is not secure. A little down the passage, the narrator admits to the persistent sense of insecurity, something he had refuted a few lines above. His incomplete safeguard has to allow him the means of escape. Though it is 'secured as anything in this world can be secured; yet someone could step on the moss or break through it . . . ' And a little further on, 'I can scarcely pass an hour in complete tranquility; at that one point in the dark moss I am vulnerable, and in my dreams I often see a greedy muzzle sniffing round it persistently' (141). The two sides of the argument persist as each – security, and means of escape in an emergency – has its own advantages and possibilities. One can be had only at the sacrifice of the other. Both the above narratives are single-voiced narratives, as is the 'Investigations of the Dog'. But all of them contain two or more arguments, born out of linguistic structure, play of ideas, oppositional reasoning and the haunting imagination of the other. To read them implies a close tying to the text, to register the many turns as they move backward and forward – quite different in nature from a labyrinth.

'The Burrow' is also about the fear of death, the sense of insecurity native to the mortal. The narrator imagines himself both as a victim and an attacker, 'A robber may very easily become my victim and a succulent one too. But I am growing old; I am not as strong as others, and my enemies are countless; it could well happen that in flying from one enemy I might run into the jaws of another' (130). The story is about fear, and the possibilities of a future which, despite its promise, threatens with annihilation. The narrator does not feel free despite the many freedoms he enjoys, simultaneously expressing the view, 'also I am not permanently *doomed* to this free life . . .' (138, emphasis mine). There is a reluctance to enter the burrow, because security would imply an abandonment of many freedoms and a descent into nothingness. After prolonged internal debate, he confesses, 'I have reached the stage where I no longer wish to have certainty' (164).

'The Burrow' is a multiple metaphor for fear and insecurity, loneliness and alienation, and the need for freedom along with security. The choices are so different and so demanding!

Jonathan Turk in an article titled 'Rituals of Dying, Burrows of Anxiety in Freud, Proust, and Kafka: Prolegomena to Critical Immunology' has described disnarration as a textual strategy of paradigmatic narration, providing antigens against imminent threats, and has commented on this disnarration and observed that the textual figure immunity can be described as analeptic prolepsis. 'The term immunity can make crucial contribution to literature theory as textual strategies of paradigmatic modern narrations are shown to provide antigenes against imminent threats' (141–56).

Born out of a similar situation of fear, insecurity and persecution was the Partition violence, which brought in its wake a great deal of writing expressing the dualities of relationships, the constant sway between the internal and the external, unsettling in its impact on human perceptions of reality. Mankind does not make a single, unified whole; the 'other' is always present, often demonised but equally vulnerable. The presence of a good Muslim or a good Hindu in these narratives is not an attempt at hope, but a depiction of the real as is the intense hatred of the 'other', a hatred combined with fear and a temporary madness. The difference is one of the human ability to distinguish or not distinguish between difference and sameness. There is a difference in the way a witness writes and the way a retrospective reconstruction, partly imagined, partly distanced, is written.

I have in mind the work of two writers – Saadat Hasan Manto and Intizar Husain;[5] and the difference in their exposition of the violence that recoils and dehumanises. Like Kafka, Manto imagines being in a wilderness. In the introduction to his collection of short stories entitled *Jungle*, there is a reference to D.H. Lawrence and a quote on the multiple self, the untamed and the dark within man wherein roaring tigers, winding snakes, white lambs, chirping birds and slippery eels are all present. At night one can hear the sound of one's own breathing. Afraid of confronting the beast within us, we show a deliberate indifference to it and pretend that it does not exist (free summing up of the editors' quotation from Lawrence). It is this dark world that Manto enters fearlessly, to explore both the anguish and the reasoning within, opening out its various layers in story after story. In many of them, such as 'Blouse' and 'Faha', he uses a sore as a metaphor for both physical and emotional ills.

Travelling over some identifiable and other unknown spaces, and inhabited by people of different religions, backgrounds and states, Manto's stories lay open a world of contrasts, contests between power and resistance, dreams and their annihilation in stark, realistic terms, often cold, and shockingly rational. They refer to metaphors of insanity and unbridled lust.

I propose to discuss two – one not so widely known, and the other oft-quoted. The first is 'Taawun', meaning a collaborative collectivity, and the second 'Toba Tek Singh'. 'Taawun' is part of *Siyah Hasiye* (Black Margins), a description which does not only refer to a dark region but also to the margins which indicate an announcement of death. Reason and violence co-habit the same area. A frail middle-aged man appropriates the leadership of a mob of agitators and leads them to the door of a house which they find locked. Advising them to break open the lock, he watches as an observer, but when they are planning to break open the door, he intervenes. He takes out a key and advises them to stay calm and orderly and divide the loot peacefully. He advocates a gentle handling of the goods, so that they are not damaged; asks them not to grab at a roll of silk but measure it and share it. All along he coaxes them into good behaviour in sharing the spoils until a huge dog bursts on the scene, a dog who answers to the name of Tiger, leading to an automatic dispersing of the crowd. A sole straggler caught in the grip of the dog asks, 'Who are you'? Prompt comes the reply, 'The owner of this house. Watch, you are about to drop the jar. It'll break'. (283).

The seriousness of the story and its hidden meaning is masked by the sudden twist when weakness is turned into strength. How do we read it: realistically or metaphorically? This leads one to ask the question whether reversal in the expected action is an act of disnarration or not. Does it or does it not cancel out the stated half, and does it form a counter narrative to the larger unwritten narrative? It also speaks volumes for the act of caring, not only for one's own self but also for inanimate objects. At the linguistic level every second sentence cancels the preceding.

'Toba Tek Singh' is so famously known that I have only a brief comment on it; a story about division and reunion, about evacuation and return and the madness of it all. By locating the narrative in a lunatic asylum and the actions and queries of the mad, a dominant reaction to trauma and uncertainty and shock is identified. The confusion is confounded when locations cannot be identified and memories are unreliable. It asks larger questions: how can division govern the human psyche? How can barbed wires be cancelled? These are the questions which the bewildered man asks when an evacuation team comes to take him away from the asylum. Where is home? How can it be allotted or shifted? His madness has reason while the rationality projected by the state act is surrounded by violence and uncertainty. Which in fact is madness?

Marquez's *Chronicle of a Death Foretold* defies every generic affiliation. Based on a real-life happening, it is also a race between factual history and imagination (Diaz-Migoyo 74–75). At one level it is a detective story turned inside out, at another it simultaneously enters into the minds of the victim as well as his attackers; at yet another level it unveils a whole culture of honour and revenge; it works like a Greek tragedy with the furies pursuing Santiago Nasar, and he is divinely unconscious of his approaching death. The novella is a layered narrative and works simultaneously with at least three different structures: first, the stepping forth of the victim; second, the still yet fleeting point of the Bishop's visit; and third, the reluctant motivation of the two killers. Caught between the aftermath of Angela Vicario's wedding and the impending visit of the Bishop, the narrative of life and death is played out in macabre terms. The investigator, in this case it could be taken as the authorial voice, carries on a personal inquiry lasting for more than twenty years – one based on memories, recalls, interviews, images, the picks on the moments of disnarration which contradict the narrative statement and comment on the blurring of realities. It appears, in hindsight, to be a collaborative crime of silences, forgotten knowledge and closed doors, a crime in which friends and enemies have come together to lead him to his death. The joy and merriment of the wedding night, the glory of the Bishop's visit and the strange pursuit interplay with each other.

On the morning of his death, Santiago Nasar, after a short restless sleep, swallows a couple of aspirins, dresses in his best clothes and while suffering from a heavy head, pronounces it a good day. Others have memories only of its gloomy funereal atmosphere. He rushes through the house, briefly telling his mother of his dreaming of birds, and the mother, an interpreter of dreams, attaches to it no significance. She tells him to carry an umbrella, but the cook, on the contrary, recalls a hot, sunny day. Victoria, the cook, and her daughter, insist that they had no knowledge of his impending death. But, in a later confession admit to having known about it. Only, they did not take it seriously. The death takes place in the first two pages but working in a triple time-scale – one of the day's happenings; second, the record of the enquires; and the third, of a later personal effort of going back to the incident to recover the remnants of its truth – the story moves to and fro, to Santiago's father, to his love relationship, to the future, the broken promises, the architecture of the house, the routine practices, the sub-lives of the personae involved in the act either through disbelief, fear or inaction, ranging from his own mother to the Mayor (18). In the meantime, all efforts to thwart Santiago Nasar's journey come to naught, and all desire of his killers to be prevented from committing the crime also come to naught.

The mysterious world of the observable 'real' has a deep equally mysterious underground leaving us with several unanswered questions. The motive is never fully gone into: was he or was he not guilty? Did Victoria Guzman keep silent because she treated it as mindless gossip or did she want them to kill him? (11) A written message left for Santiago and slipped under the door goes unnoticed (13). Images of sacrificial animals such as rabbits, cocks and goats recur in the first few pages, foretelling his fate. The investigator's sister and mother, who normally were in the know of everything, simply hadn't heard of it (19), yet a few lines later we find that Margot, the sister, asked her mother to remove the extra plate meant for Santiago as if she already knew.

The other angle of the story is Bayardo San Roman, a stranger no one likes, yet accepts. He is the bridegroom who sends back his bride, one night after a marriage she had been forced into (35). The man rode roughshod over other people's needs and feelings. A gambler, he pushed his way around. The gambler metaphor is transferred to his prospective bride and the prospective victim (40–41), the dark interiors of the mind with the potential of upsetting all known realities. Further contradictions surface. In the court trial the twins, Pablo and Pedro, admit to the killing but profess innocence. They feel no remorse. But 'the reality seemed to be that the Vicario brothers had done nothing right in line with the killing of Santiago Nasar right off and without any public spectacle, but had done much more than could be imagined for someone to stop them from killing him, and they had failed' (49) They waited for him but did not see him come out because he had taken a different exit. They announce openly to everyone (52, 54), yet no one believes them, people treated them as if they were children, or drunk, or a pair of bluffers. Their knives are taken away, but they can't be arrested just on suspicion. The authorities feel that by disarming the twins, their duty is over (61). Yet the killing does take place. The twins too are caught in this trap: 'There's no way out of this, it's as if it had already happened' (62).

The whole action is full of cancellation of known facts, of non-belief and indifference, of non-remembering and not paying attention. The doors normally kept open are found closed, and the doors opened for Santiago to come back in an emergency remain unvisited. The end itself is full of the uncalled witnesses of the past. The autopsy brings up the medal he had swallowed at the age of four and the scars of long-healed diseases, the various knife stabs, perforations and wounds like the stigma of the Cross. The emptied body is filled with rags and stitched up so that he can be buried properly in a coffin with silk quilt lining. But just the opposite happens; the body couldn't withstand any of it and 'he was in such a bad shape that it was already unbearable in the house' (7). The dead man is buried but the smell surrounds and envelops everyone. And because of the smell the killers are unable to keep their food.

Twenty-seven years later, the narrator is still trying to put the record together with details from the past, retrospective remembering and bits of forgotten happenings; there is a total lack of cause in Angela's marriage, in Santiago's killing, in Bayardo's arrival in the township – yet, all of them have obvious, stated courses. The perhaps false naming of Santiago as her seducer had also morally implicated Angela in the crime. Entering into a loveless marriage (a fact stated in the novella), the sudden termination of the marriage ends in her being mentally possessed by the man she married (92). ' "I was crazy over him", she told me, "out of my mind" ' (93). Over the years, Bayardo's presence continues to haunt the mother and daughter, until finally he comes back, fat and already bald, with a load full of her letters, unopened and unread.

Almost everything in the narrative is unclinched, rewritten, contradicted – love changes into indifference, hate into love and guilt into innocence – 'the victim's very behavior during his last hours was overwhelming proof of his innocence' (101). When he learnt of his impending death, Santiago's behaviour was the 'bewilderment of innocence' (102). Nobody takes the threats of the twins seriously, yet everybody believes that there is no use warning Santiago for, 'No matter what, he's as good as dead already' (103).

The final act of disnarration comes right at the end when the first few pages from his setting out in the early morning and having a passing conversation with his mother (4–12) is disnarrated by an alternative memory (113–17). When Flora Miguel wakes up in the morning, when Santiago pays a visit which is full of anger on Flora's side and he learns about the death sentence passed on him, his bewilderment, the efforts of Flora's father and Yamin Shaium to offer him protection. It erases all that was described earlier – the incidents, the feelings and the relationship – and it also throws light on the community's efforts to protect him, reversing not only the detective genre, but the narration of the events. These are moves into hidden motives lurking under the community's projected relationship of harmony. This final unravelling creates fresh uncertainty about motives, guilt and innocence, and ends on a note of uncertainty and irresolution.

Marquez, through this reversal, casts doubts on both epistemology and phenomenology, revealing the vulnerability of the human. Thus disnarration, which often goes unnoticed, is in actuality the uncertainty of the shifting world outside and our equally tentative and temporary grasp of it. It marks a resistance to any singular interpretation, to the certainty of rationality and to the violence outside which is difficult to cope with unless we belie it. Further, it is the interstitial spaces between narration and disnarration that allow silences to be articulated. At the level of the reader it demands an entry into the text, almost as a co-author, demanding responsibility. More often than not, it is disturbing, only very rarely giving space to humour, farce or irony. Like Penelope's web, the unravelling and the re-weaving go hand in hand. It attempts to set cultural narratives in different perspectives and rewrites history.

Marquez's act of disnarration, though confusing and circuitous, has its own rightful place in the larger narrative of life. Pierre Macherey, in his essay, 'The Text Says What it Does Not Say', problematises both silence and (dis)narration, locating them in the unknowable, 'the work does not *know* itself', a knowledge of the work is not elaborated in the work (216). Taking his argument further, he points out that 'the speech of the book comes from a certain silence, matter which is endowed with form, aground in which he traces a figure' (217). The reader's mind has necessarily to engage with the stated and the unstated, narration and disnarration and language and silence, moving out of the text in multiple, and at times opposite, directions. Yet in all this the firm anchor is in the plenitude which the text possesses.

Let me leave you with a question; what then is disnarration? A ploy, a silence, a philosophy, a dialogue or a plural narrative?

Notes

1. My reference is to the preoccupation with insanity in the early feminist criticism, which was primarily a way of symbolising — both on the writer's and the critic's part — and highlighting the isolation and the lonely struggle of the heroine. This is traceable right from *The Mad Woman in the Attic* (1979) to *The Female Malady* (1985).
2. Eccentricity, in itself, indicates non-relatedness with the very immediate, and also an inability to locate action in a cohesive world. There is, in addition to eccentricity, an indication of disjunction. Sterne's *Tristram Shandy* (1759–65) with its inner debates overflowing into outer space, his interior monologues, Cervantes' *Don Quixote* (1605–15) and, in some measure, Dickens' *Pickwick Papers* (1837), all problematise the relationship of the mind to the external, and express the disconnectedness present in the everyday act of living, as one strives to combat the present, the inherited past, and the whole demanding process of evolution of the self.

3. Cornis-Pope in his essay 'Postmodernism', comments on the radicalisation of the novel both thematically and poetically, 'taking it out of its traditional, patriarchal, rationalist and monocultural moorings'. He further proceeds to quote Barbara Christian's observation that people of color 'have always theorised . . . but in forms quite different from the Western forms of rational logic . . . our theorising . . . is often in narrative forms, in the stories we create, in riddles and proverbs, in the play with language' (183).
4. Also refer Steiner's essay, 'The Hollow Miracle' in *Language and Silence*.
5. I have not discussed Intizar Husain's stories here but refer the reader to Alok Bhalla's volume on *Stories about the Partition of India* and Husain's 'The City of Sorrow' (377–94), where a non-recognition of self is an act of disnarration.

WORKS CITED

Bhalla, Alok. Ed. *Stories about the Partition of India*. 1994. New Delhi: Harper Collins Publishers, 1999. Print.

Brod, Max. Epilogue. *The Trial*. Franz Kafka. Trans. Willa and Edwin Muir. 1935. Harmondsworth: Penguin, 1971. 252–56. Print.

Camus, Albert, *The Outsider*. Trans. Stuart Gilbert. 1942. Harmondsworth: Penguin, 1965. Print.

Connolly, Cyril. 'Introduction.' *Nineteen Eighty Four* by George Orwell. 1949. Harmondsworth: Penguin, 1962. *Modern North American Criticism and Theory*. Ed. Julian Wolfreys. Edinburgh: Edinburgh UP, 2006. 176–85. Print.

Cornis-Pope, Marcel. 'Postmodernism.' *Modern North American Criticism and Theory*. Ed. Julian Wolfreys. Edinburgh: Edinburgh UP, 2006.176–85. Print.

Christian, Barbara. 'The Race for Theory.' *CulturalCritique*, 6 (Spring 1987): 51–63. Print.

Diaz-Migoyo, Gonzalo. 'Truth Disguised: *Chronicle of a Death* (Ambiguously) *Foretold*.' In *Gabriel Garcia Marquez and the Powers of Fiction*. Ed. Julio Ortego. Austin: U of Texas P, 1988. 74–86. Print.

Dostoyevsky, Fyodor. *Notes from the Underground* (1864) and *The Double* (1846). Trans. Jessie Coulson, Harmondsworth: Penguin, 1972. Print.

Gogol Nikolai. *Dead Souls*. Trans. David Magarshack. 1961. Harmondsworth: Penguin, 1980. Print.

———. *Diary of a Madman and Other Stories*. Trans. Ronald Wilks. 1972. Harmondsworth: Penguin, 1981.17–41. Print.

Husain, Intizar. 'City of Sorrow.' *Stories about the Partition of India*. Ed. Alok Bhalla. 1994. New Delhi: Harper Collins Publishers, 1999. 377–94. Print.

Kafka, Franz. *Metamorphosis and Other Stories*. 1916. Trans. Willa and Edwin Muir. 1931. Harmondsworth: Penguin, 1977. Print.

———. 'The Great Wall of China.'*Metamorphosis and Other Stories*. 1916. Trans. Willa and Edwin Muir. 1931. Harmondsworth: Penguin, 1977. 65–82. Print.

———. 'The Burrow.' *Metamorphosis and Other Stories*. 1916. Trans. Willa and Edwin Muir. 1931. Harmondsworth: Penguin, 1977. 127–66. Print.

———. *The Trial*. 1925. Trans. Willa and Edwin Muir. 1935. Harmondsworth: Penguin, 1971. Print.

Kant, Immanuel. *The Critique of Pure Reason*. Trans. Norman Kemp Smith. London: Macmillan Palgrave, 1929. Print.

Macherey, Pierre. 'The Text Says What it Does Not Say.' *Literature in the Modern World*. Ed. Dennis Walder. Oxford: OUP in association with the Open University, 1990. 215–22. Print.

Manto, Saadat Hasan. *Dastavez* (Hindi). Edited with an Introduction by Balraj Menra and Sharad Dutt. New Delhi: Rajkamal Prakashan, 1993. 5 volumes. Vol 2. Print.

———. 'Toba Tek Singh'. *Dastavez* (Hindi). Edited with an Introduction by Balraj Menra and Sharad Dutt. New Delhi: Rajkamal Prakashan, 1993. 5 volumes. Vol 2. 192–98. Print.

———. 'Taawun.' *Dastavez* (Hindi). Edited with an Introduction by Balraj Menra and Sharad Dutt. New Delhi: Rajkamal Prakashan, 1993. 5 volumes. Vol 2. 282–83. Print.

Marquez, Gabriel Garcia. *Chronicle of a Death Foretold*. Trans. Gregory Rabassa. 1982. London: Picador. Published by Pan Books, 1983. Print.

Morrison, Toni. 'Unspeakable Things Unspoken: The Afro-American Presence in Literature.' *The Tanner Lectures on Human Values*. Michigan University, 7 Oct 1988. 123–63. Print.

Ngangom, Robin S. 'Poetry in the Times of Terror.' *Indian Literature*, 227 (May–June 2005): 168–74. Print.

Orwell, George. *Nineteen Eighty-Four*. 1949. Harmondsworth: Penguin, 1962. Print.

Steiner, George. 'The Retreat from the Word.' 1961. *Language and Silence: Essays 1958–1966*. 1967. Harmondsworth: Penguin, 1969. 31–56. Print.

———.'Silence and the Poet.' 1966. *Language and Silence: Essays 1958–1966*. 1967. Harmondsworth: Penguin, 1969. 57–76. Print.

———. 'The Hollow Miracle.' 1959. *Language and Silence: Essays 1958–1966*. 1967. Harmondsworth: Penguin, 1969. 136–51. Print.

Turk, Jonathan. 'Rituals of Dying, Burrows of Anxiety in Freud, Proust and Kafka: Prolegomena to Critical Immunology.' *Germanic Review. Literature, Culture, Theory*, 82. 2 (2007): 141–56. Web. 3 Feb 2013.

Wolfreys, Julian. 'Trauma, Testimony, Criticism.' In *Introducing Criticism at the 21st Century*. Ed. Julian Wolfreys. Edinburgh: UP, 2002.126–48. Print.

Section 2

Texts

'All Things Done Unto Edifying'

Anne Dowriche and the Play of History

DEBAPRIYA BASU

This essay will look at an unusual text written by Anne Edgcumbe Dowriche in 1589 in England. Its rather long title with attribution is important in that it indicates the text's preoccupations with the structure of its narrative. The book is called *The French historie: that is, a lamentable Discourse of three of the chiefe, and most famous bloodie broiles that haue happened in France for the Gospell of Iesus Christ. Namelie; 1 The outrage called The wining of S. Iames his Streete, 1557. 2 The constant Martirdome of Annas Burgeus one of the K. Councell, 1559. 3 The bloodie Marriage of Margaret Sister to Charles the 9. Anno 1572. Published by A. D.*[1] It attempts to recount in 2,264 lines of alternating iambic heptameters and hexameters three important incidents in the Protestant struggle in France: an attack on a Protestant prayer meeting in 1557 known as the affair of the Rue St Jacques; the trial and execution of the Protestant martyr Annas Burgeus in 1559, and the murder of the Huguenot leader Gaspard de Coligny whose death preceded the St Bartholomew's day massacre of 1572, ending with the demise of the villainous French king, which is seen as an act of God's judgement and the triumph of good over evil in the text.

Dowriche's text is based upon Jean de Serres's *Commentariorum de statu religionis & reipublicae in regno Galliae libri* (1572–75) translated by the minister Thomas Tymme as *The three partes of commentaries containing the whole and perfect discourse of the ciuill warres of Fraunce* (London, 1574, published by Frances Coldocke); François Hotman's *A true and plaine Report of the Furious outrages in Fraunce* (printed in 1573 and used by Christopher Marlowe in his *Massacre at Paris* c. 1592); Innocent Gentillet's *Discovrs, svr les moyens de bien govverner et maintenir en bonne paix vn Royaume[. . .] Contre Nicolas Machiauel Florentin* (1576) widely circulated in the manuscript

English translation of Simon Paterick called the *Contre Machievel* (first published in English in 1602 and cited by Dowriche herself), and possibly other manuscript versions of political speeches.

Anne Edgcumbe's lived experience might have contributed in no small measure to her telling of the contemporary religious turmoil in France, although, as Walter Raleigh noted, a teller of recent controversial history was likely to be struck in the teeth for her efforts at following truth 'too neare the heeles' (E4r, preface). Anne was the daughter of Sir Richard Edgcumbe (*d.* 1562) and Elizabeth Tregian, born probably a little before 1560 (her father's will of that year mentions provision for the education of Anne and her sister, and describes her as under age).[2] Elizabeth Tregian's family came of Catholic stock, and was allied in kinship to notorious recusants such as Francis Tregian, and had undergone religious persecution under Elizabeth (Sampson, 'Anne Edgcumbe/Dowriche,' 101). Her father was John Tregian who had been an important official at court, 'Esquire of the Body to Henry VIII, Steward of the Chamber and Gentleman Sewer of the King's Chamber' (Sampson, 'Anne Edgcumbe/Dowriche,' 102). The Catholic Elizabeth Tregian married Richard Edgcumbe around 1535. Both Richard Edgcumbe and his son Pearse Edgcumbe were Members of Parliament (Stevenson *et al.*, 109).[3] The manner of the education wished upon Anne in her father's will indicates that the Edgcumbe family was Protestant, and her writing, of course reveals ardent Reformist zeal, although she must have had a mixed upbringing. Julie Sampson, who has recreated a web of family relationships of the Devonshire Edgcumbes, rightly suggests that the experiential reality of Dowriche's recusant maternal family brutally persecuted during her lifetime could not have failed to have affected the writer in some way. Sampson believes that Dowriche's poem

> may well include narration of some of the events there [at the Bartholomew's Day massacre], which she [Dowriche] absorbed through talking to individuals who had been present, particularly during the turbulent days around the massacre itself. Her position at the heart of a complicated intersection of familial threads may have meant she was close to several of those individuals who were passionately engaged with the

> historical developments of the French dramas, who then related to their own responses and reactions to what they had seen. Or, possibly, she heard stories from a close relative of one of those involved. Perhaps, as a women [*sic*] recognised for her writerly and poetic gifts, she was asked to work on a narrative of the massacre. (Sampson, blog and 'Anne Edgcumbe/ Dowriche,' 101)[4]

Thus, private reading and personal experience are both probably equally responsible for the treatment of the narrative that Dowriche comes up with. This is probably what lends a subliminal ambiguity to Dowriche's position, leading to a moment of disnarration in the text. This essay will try to describe a blip in the narrative that opens up for a while a vista of good and evil as universally human categories rather than specifically Protestant and Papist ones. This is a road that is tantalisingly glimpsed but not taken, that, indeed, *cannot*, be taken in the order of things in Dowriche's textual universe. But by recognising this deviation the reader can fully appreciate the enrichment that moments of disnarration can bring to an apparently straightforward text. In order to appreciate the moment, however, one has to begin at the beginning.

The French historie's corpus is composed almost wholly of orations and speeches and bristles with marginal notes and glosses. The story of the recent atrocities in France is told in a multitude of voices, all rendered in the first person to lend immediacy to the experience. The tale is told by an Englishman who hears a mournful cry which greatly disturbs him and roots him to the spot, 'as one in traunce' (4, Br).[5] He thinks that this might be an unfortunate traveller robbed by thieves but contrary to expectation, sees '[a]llone, no peril nigh, within a bushie dale,/ A stranger sate': so, 'I got aside to heare his dolefull tale' (13–14, Br). This stranger is the Frenchman, who takes over the narrative with a monologue that sets the political background for his story. Dowriche's marginal note provides the stage directions, as it were, and announces that the ensuing passage contains '[T]he pitiful Lamentation of a godlie Frenche Exile, which for persecution forsook his Countrie' (Br). At the end of the exile's lament (which overflows with explicatory references and comments printed in the margin by Dowriche), the Englishman reveals himself to the exile and the fact is imparted to the reader embedded in the exile's monologue, 'But is that not an *English-man* that I haue yonder spide?' (102, B2v). This line is annotated with a lower case 'a' and the note is another stage direction: 'The French pilgrim hauing espied the Authour, cometh to him' (B2v). The Englishman is identified as the author, and Dowriche's voice is suppressed here but the Englishman's voice too is suppressed, giving the Frenchman's voice ultimate prominence.

As the opening pages of the poem reveal, the first remarkable thing about the text is its play with various voices, both authorial and narrative. The book's prefatory material is ostensibly in the author's voice. Indeed, the text lends itself to such exploration of narrative choice and refusal as this paper attempts precisely because the author speaks emphatically from within her own identity. As is well known, Renaissance Englishwomen were notorious misdirectors of authorial voice, but Dowriche happily doesn't shy away from attribution. There is confident use of her signature in various spellings and forms, most usually 'A D', (seven times) throughout the book, which argues for a degree of self-assurance unusual in a woman writer of the time although she does pay lip-service to the conventions of modesty and draws attention to the limitations of her gender. Although there is slim historical data about the author, her preface, dedicated to her more extensively-recorded Member of Parliament brother, confirms her identity.

In the epistle to her readers she makes her methodology clear, justifying her use of speeches and oratory for the narration of history. All the orations in her book, she says, are created imaginatively so that the villains speak as though they are given tongue by the devil (which they are, in spirit), and the speeches of the martyrs, the King, the Queen and the Guise and other characters '*marke that of purpose the nature both of the person that speaks and also the matter that is spoken, are liuely set downe*' (A4r). This is remarkable indeed because through this statement Dowriche accords verisimilitude to imagination and reveals sensitivity to literary theories from Aristotle to Sidney. Such orations are necessary, she adds, following the practice of the compilers of *The Myrrour for Magistrates* (1559), '*so that here are not bare examples of vertue and vice, but also the nature and qualities of those vertues or villainies are manifestly depainted to them that will seeke for it*' (A4r).

The poem itself adopts classical and medieval traditions of presenting history through oration,[6] and the narrative is constructed through monologues in every kind of voice of which the much-celebrated Catherine de Medici's 'Machiavel' speech is not the least striking. Satan is introduced as a character, the ostensible villain and catalyst of evil, perhaps in a convenient use of Middle English performance practice. In order to make structural sense of the narrators used in the poem both Douglas Peterson's analysis of the framework of the French *chanson d'aventure* (Peterson 1967, 18–19) and Gerald Prince's system of narratorial hierarchisation are useful. Prince anatomises narrators in the following way: '[t]he one who ultimately introduces the entire narrative (including all the mini-narratives comprising parts of it) is the main narrator. The others are secondary narrators, or tertiary ones, etc. [. . .] a tertiary narrator, for example, may be more important or interesting than a secondary one' (*Narratology*, 16). The main narrator in our text is an Englishman with markedly Protestant sympathies who begins and ends the tale; the French refugee is the secondary narrator who, nevertheless, carries the entire story on his own shoulders with the help of sundry tertiary narrators (such as the above-mentioned Satan and Catherine de Medici, who are also characters with dialogue). The point is, that although she makes it clear in prefatory material that she is the author of the work, Dowriche's voice is carefully absent within the world of the text, with one telling exception (which I see as a moment of disnarration and discuss more fully below). Her presence in her own text is very literally marginalised and can be heard only in the network of reference and gloss that she weaves around the narrative. Dowriche's voice surrounds the text and impinges upon it, instead of being assimilated within it. The authorial voice is present in the prefatory material, the numerous shoulder notes, section headings and glosses that hold the fabric of the story in place and lend it context. The text proper is the realm of the editorial voice. This voice is the super-narrator who is also the implied author whose vision gives the text its ethical charge.[7] This ethical charge is incontrovertibly activist in nature: this text, like most of Renaissance writing, seeks to teach and edify.

The French historie is a stimulating and disturbing poem. It engages energetically with issues of textuality and the methodology of textual documentation for the purposes of reporting events. It uses the double-edged sword of citation and gloss to weave a textile of texts, pulsing in constant conversation with each other, and through this it both generates and participates in a communal discourse. It is a text deeply interested in textuality although it negotiates its concerns through the conventions of orality. It uses its female authorship to take numerous liberties with form and content. It creates the earliest Machiavel figure in English literature, that too female, and whips up a prototype of the dramatic monologue. It indulges in descriptions of violence, death, mutilation and blood with a fascination and affect that is as disturbing as it is serious. It is all this, but it is more still. In the midst of the carnage and casual brutality, the text begins to sound less like mere partisan polemics. This effect is achieved through a judicious selection of material from her source author and Dowriche's stress on the editorial function becomes apparent from any comparison with Tymme's translation. A narrative refusal to conform to the reformist agenda is discernible in her departures from Thomas Tymme and it is rewarding to unearth this trail that is discovered (in the Renaissance sense of being unveiled) but not explored.

The French historie has its share of straightforward disnarrative moments, as when Catherine de Medici, exhorting her son and his advisors to decimate the reformists while dissembling friendship, exclaims, 'For heere I do protest, if I had bene a man;/ I had my selfe before this time this murder long began' (1414–15, G4r). For Prince, who analyses the concept and christens it disnarration, 'terms, phrases, and passages that consider what did not or does not take place [. . .] constitute the disnarrated, whether they pertain to the narrator's vision [. . .] or whether they relate to the vision of a character' which can comprehend 'alethic expressions of presumed impossibility or unrealized possibility [. . .], deontic expressions of (observed) prohibition, epistemic expressions of ignorance, ontologic expressions of nonexistence, purely imagined worlds, desired worlds, or intended worlds, unfulfilled expectations, unwarranted beliefs, failed attempts, crushed hopes, erroneous suppositions and false calculations, and so forth' (*Narrative as Theme*, 32). Catherine de Medici's upbraiding is more piquant, thanks to the disnarrative subjunctive she uses here.

However, narrative refusals and ruptures that push the text away from its overt agenda are even more illuminating. One interesting example of a choice not made and a possibility not actualised is a moment of rupture in the text that appears to be inadvertent. After one of the Huguenot nobles is killed, the narrator (who is the Frenchman as reported through the Englishman's speech) comments, 'This was the cruell ende of that most famous man;/ To *read* the same without remorse, I thinke no creature can' (1902–3, I3v, emphasis mine). The entire edifice of narration through reported speech, the stress on oratory and the oral nature of storytelling that the text had harped upon, crumbles. But if this is inconsistent with the poem's *spoken* purpose, it is not so with its practice. From the beginning, the editorial narrator had been prolific in commentary. By refusing to adhere to orality and erupting through the plot at this point, the authorial editor sets the mark of textuality on her narrative.

The projected readership is also problematised. On the surface the author seems to be addressing her Bible-wielding co-religionists who are also lovers of poetry: she addresses four lines of verse 'To the Reader that is friendlie to Poetrie' after having devoted more than two pages of prose in compressed italics to the 'Reader'. However, the message that the implied author is seeking to teach is logically more relevant for the persecutors of reformists, the very people that the poem and its speakers malign. The nested narrators and orators all use violent and visceral description to promote the Protestant cause and vociferously berate the Satanic villainy of Catholic kings. The villainous Catholics, too, give as good as they get but the vile acts are all theirs and therefore they lose the reader's sympathy. But the text also talks of the goodness of common people, like de Nance and 'The common hangman of Lions', (I4r, margin gloss) who are not always Protestants. After de Coligny's murder and mutilation sets off the orgy of death, the king's troops go hunting for Huguenots in every house and chamber, cutting off the heads of people who are sleeping or hiding. Even nobility is not immune. De Nance, captain of the guard, is ordered to kill the Count of Rochefoucauld, formerly on good terms with the king. He refuses the king's orders, invoking, among others, the inevitable King David story. He will not act like Joab, who killed Uriah on David's orders, because he does not wish to lose his soul. He is loyal to the king by profession and choice but he is, above all, most loyal to his own ethical code; he will not do what he considers to be wrong: 'De Nance to kill his frend no wight shall euer see,/ Though for refusall he were sure beheaded for to be' (1732–3, iv). This comparatively long oration (44 lines) for a hitherto unintroduced character sets this speech apart as important in the content of the story. The hangman of Lyons, too, expresses similar sentiments:

> For I will not defile my hands with guiltlesse blood,
> Nor giue consent (said he) to doo the thing that is not good.
> On such as are condemnde by Iustice and by law,
> I onelie am in publike place my deadlie blade to draw.
>
> (1936–39, I4r)

It is through the narrative refusal to identify completely with the reformists in moments such as these that the text acquires the authority for imparting a more universalised doctrine.

Whereas the first section of the text provides an account of generalised persecution of the godly and the martyrdom of an individual French reformist, the heart of the poem is made up of the horrors of St Bartholomew's Day that so distressed both mainland Europe and England, and gave rise to so much anti-Catholic literature, not least famous of which is Marlowe's *Massacre at Paris* (1594). It is titled '*The bloodie marriage, or butcherlie murder of the Admirall of France, and diuers other noble and excellent men, at the marriage of Margaret the Kinges owne sister, vnto Prince Henrie sonne to the Queen of Navarre, committed the 24 of August in the citie of Paris Anno 1572*' (F2r). This part has its own structure and organisation, comprising the prologue, the 'plaie' (divided into two further sub-sections) and the judgment. The prologue introduces the characters, among them many noblemen who have begun supporting the Huguenots, principal among them being Admiral de Coligny. This development disturbs Satan who marshals his servants for counsel and delineation of strategy. This would be a treacherous war, since the two preceding civil wars had shown the inefficacy of force, and victory would be assured by Machiavellian guile. The 'secret' strategy that Satan as Machiavel has in mind is to lull the reformist leaders into a false sense of security with 'louing letters, words, and cheere' (1089, F2v). The king (Charles IX) will be the chief player in every sense of the word. He will dissemble contrition and love and condemn the enemies of the Huguenots, sealing his love by the declaration of the betrothal of his own sister to Henry of Navarre. And so the fatal gathering in Paris that will lead to a frenzied shedding of blood is instituted. However, before the massacre proper begins, on the way back from a meeting on the day of this 'bloodie' (F2r) marriage Admiralde Coligny is shot at and retreats to the castle of Henry of Navarre for treatment. While under treatment, he requests a royal visit saying that he has a secret to impart concerning the safety of the king. This 'secrete' is not disclosed; it is a moment of textual silence. But the speech (1306–42 G2r) that follows warns the king of a conspiracy to 'ingraffe a strange *Italian* weede,/ Which may in France most surelie choake the Princes royall seede' (1316–17, G2v). He continues:

> This is the *onelie* wood ô King that doth mainteine the fire
> Of these your ciuill warres (although they doo *pretend*
> Religion, and some other thing) this is the chiefest end
> Of all their drift [. . .]
>
> (1318–20, G2v, *emphases mine*)

De Coligny, therefore, identifies politics and the cut-throat rivalry for political supremacy as the true cause of the religious wars. This is an eye-opening moment that slams the story out of the court of religious polemic. This is one of the nodal disnarrative moments in Dowriche's story.

Although Dowriche's poem is unabashedly reformist, de Coligny's speech to the king is part of a key to a different agenda.

Possibly what he says in the king's ear is what the implied author would have her readers hear as well. It seems unusual that a hardcore militant Huguenot should suddenly reduce the generation of two bloody and traumatic religious civil wars to exclusively political motives. The narrative insinuates that rulers use religion as a tool in the deadly game of power they play and warns against the fickleness of monarchy rather more forcibly than against the evils of papacy; and common people like de Nance and the hangman are slaughtered in this deadly play. After all, England had seen innumerable examples of kings using religion to further their own political ambitions, most blatantly in Henry VIII's antics with faith, leading to massacres no less horrifying than the one being narrated.[8]

Dowriche's text wallows in violence and dwells on gory details. But the moments of disnarration indicate that the aim of all this bloody-mindedness is to bring home to her readers the exact horror of such experiences thereby enabling them to desist in the future. Prince, in his analysis of French novels, finds that all of them take narrative as a theme. (This is also why he calls his findings *Narrative as Theme.*) For some, as in *A Thousand and One Nights*, the theme of narrating is a matter of survival. In others, such as de la Fontaine's 'La Jeune Veuve' and Camus' *La Peste*, it is 'a matter of the narrated as a source of truth' (*Narrative as Theme*, 26). In spite of the dramatic elements, oratory and fictionalisation of the story (also, perhaps, because of them), Dowriche's narrating, too, is constructed as a source of truth. With typical Renaissance publishing flair, a personified 'Truth' is visually depicted in the pair of identical woodcut emblems placed parenthetically around the body of the text with the motto 'virescit vulnere veritas' or 'truth flourishes through a wound'.[9] The female figure of truth is lashed by a disembodied hand but it cannot subdue her, 'She wounded, springs; bedeck with crowne of Peace' (line 15, last line of verse of the closing emblem at the end of the book, L2r). Peace is important not only in the context of the French wars, but also because the English victory over the Spanish Armada in 1588 is a particularly fresh issue in the public mind when Dowriche publishes her work. In this context of national peace and prosperity, de Coligny's words resonate with some dimension other than the overtly reformist. The poem talks about bloody wars at a time of peace, implying that complacence in this situation might not only be dearly bought but would be bought at the price of uncounted innocent lives sacrificed on the altar of politics in the name of religion. Keeping the sufferings of Dowriche's maternal family in mind, therefore, it might not be too amiss to see Dowriche's text as teaching against the tendency to 'quicklie finde a path to perfect peace' (H4) through indiscriminate slaughter. For all its militant Protestantism, the moments of disnarration appear to erect a strong bias against religious persecution in *general* rather than persecution against Protestants in particular. In its play with texts, Anne Dowriche makes her revisionist historical narrative select its playmates and players carefully not only to edify the reformist zealot who is her overt narratee but also to move to tolerance and humanity the flesh and blood individual, irrespective of gender, class or religious persuasion, who dwells beneath.

Notes

1. This is STC (2nd edition) 7159, held at the Huntington Library, the facsimile of which is published in Woods *et al.* This is my working text and is subsequently referred to as *The French historie* in this essay.
2. This essay follows the biography by Patrick Cullen provided in the Facsimile edition and the revised *Oxford Dictionary of National Biography* entry, 'Dowriche, Anne (*d.* in or after 1613)' by Kate Aughterson. See also Stevenson et al. for a recent biographical account. See also Robin et al., 115, for a short biographical note.
3. No source cited. This is the Pearse to whom Dowriche dedicates her work.
4. Also relevant for understanding Dowriche's relations with other women writers is White's valuable research into literary circles of women based upon what she calls 'prioritizing geographical locality and seeking to excavate a region's literary, religious, and kinship networks' (189). White's investigations have revealed surprising connections with other literary women deeply committed to the reformist cause, not least among them Anne Vaughan Locke (author of probably the first sonnet sequence in English, 'A Meditation of A Penitent Sinner,' 1560).

5. I use continuous line numbering in parentheses following the text printed in Wynne-Davies ed. but also provide signature numbers of STC (2nd Edition) 7159 as published in Woods et al. for consistency. For marginalia only folio number is indicated. Recto and verso are indicated by lowercase 'r' and 'v' after the folio signature.
6. For discussions of Renaissance historiography see, among others, Levy, Burke, Collingwood, Cochrane and Kewes.
7. Although the terms 'implied author' (IA) and 'super-narrator' are no longer dependent on citations, for IA see Booth, for super-narrator see Parr, '*Don Quixote*: An Anatomy of Subversive Discourse', '*Don Quixote*: The Quest for a Superreader and a Supernarratee' and 'On Narration and Theory.'
8. See Bucholz, Loewenstein and Shagan among others for state-sanctioned religious violence in Renaissance England.
9. Interestingly, the same emblem was embroidered by Mary, Queen of Scots in what later came to be known as the Oxburgh Hanging. See Sampson, 'Anne Edgcumbe/Dowriche,' 134.

WORKS CITED

Aughterson, Kate. 'Dowriche, Anne (*d.* in or after 1613).' *Oxford Dictionary of National Biography*. Ed. H. C. G. Matthew and Brian Harrison. Oxford: Oxford UP, 2004; online ed. Oct. 2006. Web. 14 June 2011. <http://0-www.oxforddnb.com.catalogue.ulrls.lon.ac.uk/view/article/7987>.

Booth, Wayne C. *The Rhetoric of Fiction*. Chicago: U of Chicago P, 1965. Print.

Bucholz, R. O. and Newton Key. *Early Modern England, 1485–1714: A Narrative History*. Malden, MA: Blackwell Publishing, 2004. Print.

Burke, Peter. *The Renaissance Sense of the Past*. London: Edward Arnold, 1969. Print.

Cochrane, Eric. 'The Profession of the Historian in the Italian Renaissance.' *Journal of Social History* 15 (1981): 51–72. Print.

Collingwood, R. G. *The Idea of History*. T. M. Knox ed. Oxford: Clarendon Press, 1946. Print.

Cullen, Patrick. 'Introduction.' Susanne Woods, Betty S. Travitsky and Patrick Cullen eds. *The Early Modern Englishwoman: A Facsimile Library of Essential Works, Series I, Printed Writings, 1500–1640*. Part 2, vol. 10, *The Poets, I: Isabella Whitney, Anne Dowriche, Elizabeth Melville [Colville], Aemilia Lanyer, Rachel Speght, Diana Primrose, Anne, Mary and Penelope Grey*. Aldershot, Hants: Ashgate, 2001. xi–xiii. Print.

Demers, Patricia. *Women's Writing in English: Early Modern England*. Toronto: U of Toronto P, 2005. Print.

Dowriche, Anne. *The French historie: that is, a lamentable Discourse of three of the chiefe, and most famous bloodie broiles that haue happened in France for the Gospell of Iesus Christ. Namelie; 1. The outrage called The wining of S. Iames his Streete, 1557. 2. The constant Martirdome of Annas Burgeus one of the K. Councell, 1559. 3. The bloodie Marriage of Margaret Sister to Charles the 9. Anno 1572*. Published by A. D. London: Thomas Orwin for Thomas Mann, 1589. Print.

Kewes, Paulina. 'History and its Uses.' Ed. Paulina Kewes. *The Uses of History in Early Modern England*. San Marino, California: Huntington Library, 2006. 1–30. Print.

Levy, F. J. *Tudor Historical Thought*. Huntington Library, 1967. Toronto: U of Toronto P, 2004. Print. Renaissance Society of America Reprint Text Series.

Loewenstein, David. *Treacherous Faith: The Specter of Heresy in Early Modern English Literature and Culture*. Oxford: Oxford UP, 2013. Print.

Parr, James A. '*Don Quixote*: The Quest for a Superreader and a Supernarratee.' *Ciber Letras* 4: n. pag. Web. 2 Feb. 2013. <http://www.lehman.cuny.edu/ciberletras/v04/Parr.html>

———. 'Don Quixote: An Anatomy of Subversive Discourse.' Juan De La Cuesta Hispanic Monographs, 1988. Print. Hispanic Monographs Ser. 8.

———. 'On Narration and Theory.' *Cervantes: Bulletin of the Cervantes Society of America*, 24.2 (2004–2005): 119–35. Print.

Peterson, Douglas L. *The English Lyric from Wyatt to Donne: A History of the Plain and Eloquent Styles*. Princeton, N. J.: Princeton UP, 1967. Print.

Prince, Gerald. *Narratology: The Form and Functioning of Narrative*. Berlin: Mouton Publishers, 1982. Print. Janua Linguarum, Series Maior 108.

———. *Narrative as Theme: Studies in French Fiction*. Lincoln: U of Nebraska P, 1992. Print.

Raleigh, Walter. *History of the World*. London: Walter Burr, 1614. Print.

Robin, Diana, Anne R. Larsen, and Carole Levin. Eds. *Encyclopedia of Women in the Renaissance: Italy, France and England*. California: ABC-Clio Inc., 2007. Print.

Sampson, Julie. 'Anne Dowriche /Edgcumbe's "The French Historie" and its Westcountry Connections.' *Scrapblog: a Writer from the South-West*. Web. 09 September 2011. <http://scrapblogfromthesouth-west.blogspot.com/2011/01/anne-dowricheedgcumbes-french-historie.html>.

———. 'Anne Edgcumbe/Dowriche and *The French Historie* (2 parts).' *Devonshire Association Transactions*, 141 (2009): 93–152. Print.

Shagan, Ethan H. *The Rule of Moderation: Violence, Religion and the Politics of Restraint in Early Modern England*. Cambridge: Cambridge UP, 2011. Print.

Stevenson, Jane and Peter Davidson. Eds. *Early Modern Women Poets (1520–1700): An Anthology*. Oxford: Oxford UP, 2001. Print.

White, Micheline. 'Women Writers and Literary–Religious Circles in the Elizabethan West Country: Anne Dowriche, Anne Lock Prowse, Anne Lock Moyle, Ursula Fulford, and Elizabeth Rous.' *Modern Philology* 103.2 (November 2005): 187–214. Print.

Woods, Susanne, Betty S. Travitsky and Patrick Cullen. Eds. *The Early Modern Englishwoman: A Facsimile Library of Essential Works, Series I, Printed Writings, 1500–1640:* Part

2, vol. 10. *The Poets, I: Isabella Whitney, Anne Dowriche, Elizabeth Melville [Colville], Aemilia Lanyer, Rachel Speght, Diana Primrose, Anne, Mary and Penelope Grey*. Aldershot, Hants: Ashgate, 2001. Print.

Wynne-Davies, Marion. Ed. *Women Poets of the Renaissance*. New York: Routledge, 1999. Print.

Politics of Representing Gender Violence

Jyotirmoyee Devi's *The River Churning*

Paulomi Chakraborty

The plot of Jyotirmoyee Devi's 1967 novel *Epar Ganga, Opar Ganga – The River Churning*[1] – begins amidst the brutal communal violence of Noakhali in 1946. The protagonist of the novel, Sutara, a Hindu-Bengali girl, of about fifteen, along with her parents and elder sister, is attacked at their home by a Muslim mob. Sutara remains the only survivor of the four. This is how the night and the attack on the women of the family is narrated to us:

> Sutara stared after her [mother] when suddenly she heard her sister scream and fall to the ground. From near the shed where Mother was wrenching the flap door open she heard a shrill cry. 'I'm coming,' she called. But she could not make it. Dark shadowy figures surrounded her, some tried to grab her by the hand. Breaking free, she rushed to the pond at the back and jumped into the water. In the light of the spreading fire everything was now visible. One of the ruffians went after Mother but another stopped him, 'leave her, it's their mother, let her go.' But Didi did not stir. Was she dead? What happened to Didi? Sutara couldn't tell. She wanted to reach mother and began to run, but stumbled and fell. Then everything went blank. (8)

What happened to Sutara from this moment to her regaining consciousness several days later in the house of her rescuer Tamij Saheb, her father's friend, is not narrated in the novel. Indeed, what 'actually' happens to Sutara is cognitively unavailable not only to the readers and other characters, but even to Sutara herself.

It is possible that Sutara is raped, but we do not know this for sure. There is a brief mention by the narrator that 'she was so shattered physically and psychologically that she couldn't get up from her bed' (10). After regaining consciousness, Sutara herself keeps asking: 'Did she fall to the ground or was she pushed down?

What happened after that?' (16). Only Moinu, the youngest son of Tamij Saheb, who is the only one in the family young enough to not understand the taboo on the topic, gives Sutara a few more details once:

> 'Sutaradi, did they thrash you badly?' [Moinu] asked, 'it was a good thing Fakir came and told father. That is how Baba and Aziz bhaisaheb took our Habibullah and some other farm hands armed with cudgels and spears and carried you home. You were lying half-dead. Aziz bhai and others lifted you on their shoulders and brought you here. Fakir told us that they had beaten you badly.' (17)

Tamij Saheb's daughter, and Sutara's childhood friend, Sakina, immediately interrupts, demanding that Moinu 'stop the nonsense'. Their mother rushes in with a more soothing explanation: 'The sight of the fire and all those ruffians was too much for you. You fainted. Then you had an attack of fever just from shock. But you are going to be all right now' (17). An adult Aziz, Tamij's elder son, later remembers this night and speaks of finding Sutara as 'a bundle of clothes [. . .] lying in a pool of blood' (100). Beyond these fragmentary details, no other specifics of the assault on Sutara are disclosed.

In this paper, I propose to read the silence in the novel about what happens to Sutara on that eventful night as an instance of critical disnarration, which seeks to problematise a normative 'rape narrative' and expose the patriarchal codes of representation that often underwrite such narratives. I will broadly argue that *The River Churning* radicalises the discourse of 'violence on women' and disrupts the representative economy of 'female chastity' that lies at the bottom of a patriarchal sexual economy. The novel, we find, does not only register one kind of patriarchal violence, which is what is done to Sutara by men of the 'other community.' This 'event' occupies the relatively brief first section of the novel. The novel also brings under scrutiny – in the much longer second section of the novel – her rejection as a 'polluted woman' once she reaches Calcutta as an orphaned refugee, seeking shelter in the well-to-do, caste-Hindu household of her brother's in-laws.

What is under critique in the novel, then, is what Jasodhara Bagchi aptly describes as 'the dual control exercised by patriarchy,' in which 'riot victims like Sutara are hit twice by patriarchy: first by a male of one community who establishes his own "identity" by exercising his territoriality over her body, second by her "own" community which invokes compulsions of ritual purity to exclude her from the ritually pure domains of hearth and marriage, and drinking water' (xxxii). The ingredients of this novel are the same as those in the patriarchal narratives of female chastity/honour, but the novel becomes interventional by changing the narrative function of these ingredients. It attempts to insert a violated woman herself at the psychological–social *centre* of the narrative in contrast to patriarchal narratives *about* female honour which function by reducing the wronged woman as a mere citation of patriarchal concerns. I read the novel's narrative choice of critical disnarration as a formal strategy that enables the novel to push itself to this end. I will also argue that the act of disnarration in the novel aligns itself with a critique of the everyday violence of patriarchy, framing women's lives even in ordinary times that this novel offers. I will explore here how the novel, in the task of representing gendered violence of Partition in continuum with the historical everyday of women, probes, questions, reflects on, and confronts the limits of the language accessible to a member, also gendered, of a certain linguistic community.

Almost all critics read that sexual violence – possibly rape – took place, but have noted the deliberateness of the efforts of the narrator to keep the details ambiguous, to speculate on the reason that animated this decision to disnarrate sexual assault. Mookerjea-Leonard argues that there is no scope for reading the 'unspoken' by the author/narrator as an act of uncritical shame or as a 'residual prudery of a post-Victorian novelist': the Bangla equivalent of the word 'rape' occurs quite often in Jyotirmoyee Devi's writing, especially in her essays. Mookerjea-Leonard's argument is that the details of the assault on Sutara are omitted because the 'veiling of a bodily trauma through language constitutes a counter-discourse to the economy of display of woman' (41). A similar conclusion is also to be found in Bagchi. Bagchi describes Sutara's assault at the hand of her ' "own" community', the proverbial 'second rape', as 'a prolonged and unbearable panopticist gaze by the community over Sutara's body and mind' (xxxii). If the novel is a critique of the 'panopticist gaze', then it is pertinent that the narrative itself should refuse to allow the readers' gaze to dwell on Sutara's body. In a similar vein, describing the goal of her project, of which a reading on *The River Churning* is a part, Jill Didur has said that it sought to 'redirect the gaze of the reader/researcher away from women's bodies and sexuality', that are sites always under surveillance of community and state anyway (13).

While Mukherjea-Leonard has argued that by keeping silent on the details of the assault the novel 'recovers something of the private pain that women suffered' (41), in contrast, Jill Didur contends that we, the readers, should not imaginatively fill in the gap. Didur argues that our refusal to 'recover' what is signalled by the omission is also analogous to this realisation: we should accept the ambiguity as such and not take it for granted that the rape did, in fact, take place. 'These silences and ambiguities in women's stories', she argues, 'should not be resolved, accounted for, unveiled, or recovered, but, rather, understood as women's inability to subsume their experience within projects of patriarchal modernity that has produced them in the first place' (11). She, thus, critiques any imperative to 'recover', and sees the silence in *The River Churning* as precisely the refusal to do so. Instead, Didur argues that we should treat 'loss as loss' as Spivak has suggested (Spivak 217; qtd in Didur 136). For Didur, the silence of the author is analogous to 'the novel's refusal to "recover" Sutara's experience within the script dictated by patriarchal nationalism' (19).

The reading of the critical disnarration of rape in *The River Churning* that I offer in this paper builds on the existent commentary that I have outlined above in two ways. First, it examines the novel's attempt to problematise a normative 'rape narrative' and expose the patriarchal codes of representation that contains rape narratives; and, second, it takes the discussion on gendered silence in the direction of the role of the audience in constituting that silence. Both these readings converge on my argument about the significance of the social in *The River Churning*. Together, they aim to show how the novel brings the traumatic story of an individual refugee woman to the realm of the collective and the historical, and connect it with the violence that the everyday lives of women in patriarchy are marked with.

1

The River Churning works in a readable relation to, but radicalises, classic rape narratives. In order to demonstrate how the novel adheres to and radically differentiates itself from normative rape narratives, we have to ask how the meta-textual silence – the ambiguity about rape – fares in this consideration. As such and in itself, we cannot hail silence or ambiguity about sexual assault as the quintessential mark of feminist politics of representation. Writing on the issue of the raped woman as a subject of a narrative in the chapter, 'Life after Rape: Narrative, Rape and Feminism' in her book, *Real and Imagined Women: Gender, Culture and Postcolonialism*, Rajeswari Sunder Rajan has shown that silence on rape in the heart of a narrative need not constitute, in fact can be strongly oppositional to, feminist politics (64–82). She argues that such narrative strategies can completely undercut the purported aim of the narrative to critique the gendered injustice a raped woman is subjected to. Sunder Rajan writes:

> A feminist 'thematics of liberation,' as Teresa de Lauretis has cautioned, is insufficient to counter the forces of masculine desire that invests all narrative. This is why feminist texts of rape must also engage in textual strategies to counter narrative determinism. Such negotiations are achieved by and result in alternative structure of narrative. (73)

Sunder Rajan takes *Clarissa* and *A Passage to India* to task because 'at the centre of the narrative is only absence. Neither of the novels actually represent the scene of rape' (74). She then goes on to read these 'silence[s] at the heart of the text' (74–75) as a mystification of their actual occurrences:

> In his essay on *Clarissa*, Terry Eagleton has argued that rape itself is unrepresentable because the 'real' of the woman's body marks 'the outer limits of all language'. This, it appears to me, is part of the male mystique built around rape (as around childbirth). Such narrative theory fetishizes rape as a limit of narrative, to be tested over and over. (74)

The second reason Sunder Rajan suspects the narrative silence is that in the two canonical texts that she discusses, there is a 'deep underlying male fear that rape could be a female lie, or fiction.' As

Clarissa is 'a great proto-feminist novel, and *A Passage to India* [. . .] a major treatment of liberal humanism', one may expect them to be 'unequivocal about an act of male sexual aggression on a woman' (75). Nevertheless, for Sunder Rajan, their silence about rape is a 'symptom' of 'their reliance upon, and doubt about, the woman's "unsupported word" about her ordeal'. Sunder Rajan's reading of the feminist narrative of rape is, that in it, in contrast to the above, 'the fact of rape—even if not its graphic representation—is acknowledged in stark, brute terms, as the very premise upon which the narrative is built' (76).

This argument is, of course, of critical importance for *The River Churning*. Is the narrative strategy of *The River Churning* normative when it posits what happened to Sutara in the realm of silence? Is the mystery around whether Sutara was raped congruent to the mystification of 'the fact of rape' in *A Passage to India*: does it mystify rape by positing it as unrepresentable? I would argue that trying to represent the incident would have been far more normative for *The River Churning*. In denying that information, there is a critique of the lack of validity of precisely that category that Sunder Rajan cites as 'the woman's "unsupported word" '.

The conundrum that *The River Churning* presents is a dramatic reversal of the usual situation when a rape victim claims that she has been raped and is not believed. The trauma of this moment, which has been described many times as the 'second rape', 'as raped women have again and again testified', is intense (Sunder Rajan 76). The chastity-based economy in a caste-Hindu, Brahminical context, however, further complicates what constitutes sexual/partiarchal violence. In this context, a woman is 'feared' by the society, effectively accused, to have been raped. The fear of pollution of the purity–chastity of the woman incites an equally painful ordeal for the 'feared–raped' woman. Hindu myths have notions of, as Sunder Rajan writes, 'trials like [those of] Ahalya and Sita that seem necessary to absolve the "raped" subject of "guilt",' to 'mark her fitness for re-entry into social and moral domain' (76). Jyotirmoyee Devi has written over and over again about the injustice that Ahalya[2] and Sita[3] (and many other mythic women) suffer. Sita had to prove that she was not raped and Ahalya that she was 'innocent' when she is raped. The case of Sutara is akin to that of Sita if the silence of the text indicates that rape did not take place. If Sutara had claimed to have not been raped, no one would have believed her because she had been at the centre of a Hindu–Muslim riot and had spent days in a Muslim household. If she *had* been raped, then the silence of the text indicates the impossibility of talking about it, and her case is like that of Ahalya.

In fact, what she might have said mattered very little. She could have neither proven nor disproven rape, and in any case, the 'punishment' she receives would have been just the same on either account. Jyotirmoyee Devi's refusal to give that detail of Sutara's assault should be read as a comment on and critique of the social Brahminical norms in treating their 'soiled' (raped or not) women. The novel's refusal to give details of the degree of molestation Sutara suffers (whether or not it can constitute 'rape') foregrounds the double-bind of the either raped or 'feared raped' I described above. For us, the readers, the critical judgement of this patriarchal violence should also function, therefore, irrespective of the actual rape. As Didur has argued, 'by refusing to fill the gap in Sutara's story, Jyotirmoyee Devi's novel denies the reader "the evidence" he or she needs to assess whether or not Sutara was sexually polluted and instead redirects "our" attention to the patriarchal rationale that informs the construction of women's sexuality as polluted or pure' (155).

I will further my point by making use of an example used by Sunder Rajan herself. Writing on Jonathan Kaplan's film *The Accused*, as a case where a feminist theme is undermined by a normative narrative, Sunder Rajan criticises the film's use of the narrative device of the flashback to actually re-present the scene of rape:

> In an attempt to replicate the court's search to know whether the rape 'really' happened, the film succumbs to the device of the flashback, a device available *only* to the narrative (and never to any court of law, however sedulously it may try to recreate the scene of crime). By replaying the scene of rape, it once again makes it central to the narrative, 'the climax' of the graph of its linear structure. If the absence of the scene of rape at the heart of a narrative (as in *Clarissa* or *A Passage to India*) serves to mystify its actual occurrence, the brutal

> naturalism of its cinematic representation in *The Accused* provides a confirmation that enforces the same conclusion: the 'unsupported word' of a raped woman cannot represent rape. (75; emphasis in the original)

Using the above example, I read the absence at the heart of Jyotirmoyee Devi's text as a decision to *not* take advantage of a device 'available only to the narrative'. The text tests the reception of women like Sutara by their society and simultaneously by the readers. Sutara's contemporary society and the modern society hardly ever trust a 'woman's "unsupported word"'. The novel critiques this characteristic of patriarchal society by refusing to give evidence. Simultaneously, the novel critiques our – the readers' – desire to not trust a woman's silence, as well as our desire to probe the details so that we can then judge her or assess the treatment she receives.

In any case, as I argued above, the question of whether Sutara is actually raped or not is a cognitive cul-de-sac for her society, and us, because of the profound irony that the facticity of her rape is of little consequence. Brahmin households would still reject her as they had rejected the mythical Sita or Ahalya. In the Brahminical world view, 'rape' is not male violence on a female body but a violation – indeed the possibility of violation – of sexual chastity of a caste-Hindu female body. Sutara, the refugee woman in the new India, is 'always-already' a rape victim because she has got caught in a Partition riot and, to make matters worse, has been rescued and given shelter by Muslims. In this regard, the truth of the rape is irrelevant. What is relevant, and under critique in *The River Churning*, is the way a woman is judged for being vulnerable to this rape.

On other occasions, if we judge *The River Churning*'s narrative strategy along this line of arguments made by Sunder Rajan, we will find that it is 'alternative' and at par with the intended 'thematics of liberation' on several accounts (Sunder Rajan 73). For instance, in *The River Churning* the rape is not at the climax of the plot as in the classical masculinist rape-narratives (as for example in *Clarissa* and *A Passage to India*). *The River Churning* makes 'the structural location of the rape incident at the beginning of a woman's story', which Sunder Rajan reads as a way to get to a liberated narrative structure: 'the position of the rape scene at the beginning pre-empts expectation of its late(r) occurrence. Not only is the scene of rape diminished by this positioning but it is also granted a more purely functional purpose in the narrative economy, and narrative interest becomes displaced upon what follows' (73).

Sunder Rajan gives the examples of Alice Walker's *The Colour Purple* and Maya Angelou's *I Know why the Caged Bird Sings*, to point out that in these texts '[t]he development of the female subject's "self" begins after the rape and occupies the entire length of the narrative' (73). The readers will note that this is also the case with *The River Churning*. Here, too, there is a complete subversion of the 'recognition that desire is built upon the prolongation of suspense and the postponement of climax' (Sunder Rajan 73). Arriving at a comparable conclusion, Mookerjea-Leonard has also argued that 'the event of the assault that ruptures women's "good" past lives from the tainted present and future is not [intended to be] central to the narrative' (41). I therefore read the novel as one that problematises a rape narrative. The most central political point to such narrative is the critique of the reader or the audience of the narrative as well as of the society within which the victim is situated.

2

The silence at the heart of the novel in relation is a critical comment, I would argue therefore, on the role of its audience, largely defined, and not just the silence of the protagonist/narrator. In a prefatory 'Author's Note', Jyotirmoyee Devi, referring to a book appearing towards the end of the epic *Mahabharata*, the 'Stree Parva' (The Book/Chapter of Women), writes: 'The crux of the matter is that even the great Vedavyash could not write what is implied by the title.' And, later in the note, 'The language for it has yet to be fashioned, so naturally Stree Parva does not figure anywhere . . . ' (xxiv–xxxv). The 'Author's Note', thus, points to the violence to which women are subjected because of their gender, the absence of 'women's' part in documented collective memory (for instance, as history or canonical literature), and the difficulty – even impossibility – and the struggle of filling the gap.

Explaining the absence of 'Stree Parva', what the author cites is a fundamental lack: she says a language in which such violence can be represented 'is yet to be fashioned'. What *The River Churning* marks is not a failure of knowledge, but the failure of socially possible and permissible language. As the novel shows from the standpoint of the marginal refugee woman, this possibility or permissibility of available language is sharply gendered. This resonates with the findings about gendered trauma and silence within Partition studies. Foundational scholarship by Urvashi Butalia, Ritu Menon and Kamla Bhasin, Das, and Gyanendra Pandey has repeatedly and emphatically pointed to the fact that not only did gender structure victimhood during the Partition, but that gender *also* plays a crucial role in the resultant silence that follows the trauma.

Thus, I wish to underscore silence as a relationship of power between the speaker, whose 'absence' of speech constitutes the silence – and the listener or reader – the audience whose 'absence' or refusal of listening can equally well constitute silence. My argument about the silence of the victim in *The River Churning* is that it is as much constituted by the impossibility of speech by the speaker as it is by suppression of speech by the community within which the speaker resides. In other words, the linguistic failure of the victim is also equally a failure of the linguistic community. When Jyotirmoyee Devi writes that the 'language for it is yet to be fashioned', she is offering a critique of the social. The critique is, thus, not restricted to the violent time of the Partition alone but also extends to the larger social and historical world that preceded and follows the 'event' of the Partition. This analysis aims to develop our understanding of silence not in opposition, but further, in a different direction than our usual understanding of the silence as being silence of a *speaker*.

The departure of *The River Churning* from its narrative conventions to be silent on the details of the assault on Sutara, thus, both offers a critique of the linguistic community – within which a language to tell Sutara's story without participating in the violence against her is not possible – and participates in a radical concept of communication that we can call feminist. The radical concept of communication is to consciously move away from the kind of communication that depends on, and facilitates a hierarchical power structure between the speaker and the listener/interlocutor. In the chapter on communication, titled "'Speaking to . . . ' and 'Speaking with . . . ,' " in her book, *Feminist Thought: Androcentricism, Communication and Objectivity*, Shefali Moitra outlines and analyses the 'speaking with' pattern of communication. The participants of this kind of communication have to agree to a power-sharing rather than opting for power as domination.

The concept of 'speaking with' opens up ways we can receive a tale like that of Sutara's or a novel like *The River Churning*. What the 'speaking with' model of communication does is to put the responsibility of receiving a difficult narrative on the audience as much as on the speaker to tell such a tale. The 'speaking with . . . ' mode invites a different form of listening from us than in the standard practice of 'speaking to'.[4] The 'speaking with' form of communication, where listening plays a key role, is a radical feminist practice, and it is, of course, a critical practice that needs to be distinguished from practices of cognitive certainty, uncritical empathy or sympathy felt by the audience through identification with the victim.[5] Thus, when we use this awareness of 'speaking with', distinct from the mainstream mode of 'speaking to,' in a discussion of *The River Churning* we arrive at some insight on what Jyotirmoyee Devi's novel seeks to articulate.

The 'unspoken' of the novel illuminates the narrative politics. By remaining silent at a critical moment, the novel essentially matches Sutara's silence with its own silence. Moitra states that '[i]n "speaking with", silence is a corollary of listening. Listening entails a communicative role of silence. Listening is not confined to codified sources of meaning . . . It is only when we are silent that we begin to notice the muteness of deprived groups' (99). The task Moitra indicates by 'our silence', is the task *The River Churning* performs. The author/narrator conditions us (the readers) to be quiet so that 'we' can hear the inability of a marginalised character such as Sutara to speak.

The silence of the narrator in the text draws attention to the fact that, in spite of the commitment to speak (on part of the author, as in this novel), there is no available language in the gendered 'everyday' world. As Didur argues, 'the silence in women's accounts of sectarian violence that accompanied partition' is a 'sign of their inability to find a language to articulate their experience without invoking metaphors of purity and pollution' (11). Analogously, for a narrator who wants to narrate the story of a refugee woman, a gendered victim of the Partition, there is a similar lack of language that is not corrupted by the metaphors of purity and honour. Thus, the novel cannot just tell, but has to *show* the failure of language to represent experiences of the kind Sutara has. Indeed, the function of this disnarration is very important: the silence is to record that there is no available 'language' to talk about it. The author/ narrator is thus making a larger point of not having the linguistic space in history to talk about gender crimes. The narrative can only perform the loaded failure of social language and how deep hegemony and 'shame' thwart women from asking/answering/ uttering *anything* even when they know the truth about gender crimes.

The critique of representative impossibilities that the novel advocates is based, I have tried to show above, on a socio-political understanding of language and silence. Thus, while making trauma narrative entirely gendered, my critique also makes trauma narratives and their representative possibility/impossibility a larger political question. Through its act of disnarration, the novel brings critical focus on the role of the audience/reader/society at large in the ways women's ordinary 'everyday' lives, not just during but also beyond traumatising events of the Partition. In making silence a crucial part of its own narrative strategy, the novel tries to match the silence of the protagonist–victim with its own and allow for an ideological critique of patriarchy.

Keeping in view the importance I have attached to the communicative – hence the socio-political and emphatically gendered – aspect of trauma and silence, I have read the novel's stylistic decisions also in terms of an attempt to problematise a 'rape narrative.' This has allowed me to plot gender violence not only as a mark of the extraordinary political upheaval of the Partition, but also as a mark of the patriarchal violence of the everyday. In my reading of the novel, the critique that the novel provides is strongly addressed to the everyday.

Notes

1. For the most part I shall be using the English translation of the novel by Enakshi Chatterjee, titled *The River Churning: A Partition Novel,* so I shall be referring to the novel as *The River Churning* in this paper.
2. The story of Ahalya goes thus: Ahalya was the wife of a devout sage, Gautama. The god Indra once, disguised as her husband, made love to Ahalya. Although Ahalya had knowingly only participated in marital sex, Gautama turned her into stone as a punishment. Years later, Rama lifted the spell by touching her and persuaded her husband to forgive her. If we read the myth from a feminist perspective, we will see that there is an instructive confusion between marital sex and rape. Readers who can read Bangla should read the story 'Ahalya, Draupadi, Tara' by Jyotirmoyee Devi.
3. Sita, of course, has to walk through fire unscathed to prove her chastity after she is rescued by Rama. After returning to Ayodhya, some people raise doubts about her chastity, and Rama asks her to repeat her walk through fire again, which she refuses and chooses self-banishment.
4. This thought on power-sharing communication is shared by listener-sensitive scholarship on trauma. For example, in the context of the Holocaust, Shoshana Felman and Dori Laub's book *Testimony: Crises of Witnessing in Literature, Psychoanalysis and History* focuses on the role of the audience in 'witnessing' a historical traumatic event of the dimension of the Holocaust. The first chapter by Dori Laub titled, 'Bearing Witness or the Vicissitudes of Listening' is especially devoted to the act of listening. In this chapter, in a discussion of the 'hazards of listening', Dori Laub lists how certain defensive-mechanisms by the listener can shut down a trauma narrative (72–73).
5. 'Speaking with', thus, resonates with the arguments of Cathy Caruth in *Unclaimed Experience: Trauma, Narrative, and History* and a host of other scholarship in the field of Holocaust studies, which draws attention to the impossibility of the audience to ever 'know' fully. From a different angle, a part of this scholarship has also questioned the ethicality of the straightforwardness of the identification with the victim, which the discussions of the role of the audience and the role of listening by Shoshana Felman and Dori Laub in *Testimony* leave unquestioned. Marianne Hirsch's study of 'postmemory' has analysed the projective fantasies in the

reception of iconic images of the Holocaust. Hirsch argues that the images of child victims lure the audience into an unproblematic universalising and homogenising witnessing.

Susannah Radstone has gone further by taking into account Hirsch's attempt to arrive at a more ethical witnessing, but she cautions against the ethics of 'identification' with victimhood itself. 'Taking as its case-study Marianne Hirsch's writing on the ethical aesthetics of postmemorial photography', in Radstone's own words, she 'concludes that recent work on trauma and testimony fails to acknowledge that identification may straddle victimhood and perpetration. The acknowledgement is only possible when some containment of aggression feels possible' (59).

As an alternative mode of relating to the trauma victim available to others, Dominick LaCapra formulates the concept of 'emphatic unsettlement' in *Writing History, Writing Trauma*. 'Emphatic unsettlement' is an ethical form of affective involvement that entails 'being responsive to the traumatic experience of others, notably of victims' in a way that is not 'the appropriation of their experiences. [...] Empathic unsettlement poses a barrier to closure in discourse and places in jeopardy harmonizing or spiritually uplifting accounts of extreme events from which we attempt to derive reassurance or a benefit' (41–42).

WORKS CITED

Bagchi, Jasodhara. 'Introduction.' *The River Churning: (Epar Ganga Opar Ganga) A Partition Novel*. By Jyotirmoyee Devi. Trans. Enakshi Chattejee. New Delhi: Kali for Women, 1995. xxv–xxxiii. Print.

Butalia, Urvashi. *The Other Side of Silence: Voices from the Partition of India*. New Delhi: Penguin Books India, 1998. Print.

Caruth, Cathy. *Unclaimed Experience: Trauma, Narrative, and History*. Baltimore : Johns Hopkins UP, 1996. Print.

Das, Veena. *Critical Events: An Anthropological Perspective on Contemporary India*. Delhi: Oxford UP, 1995. Print.

Devi, Jyotirmoyee. *The River Churning: A Partition Novel*. Trans. Enakshi Chattejee. New Delhi: Kali for Women, 1995. Print.

Didur, Jill. *Unsettling Partition: Literature, Gender, Memory.* Toronto; Buffalo; London: U of Toronto P, 2006. Print.

Felman, Shoshana and Dori Laub. *Testimony: Crises of Witnessing in Literature, Psychoanalysis and History.* New York: Routledge, 1992. Print.

Hirsch, Marianne. 'Family Pictures: *Maus,* Mourning, and Post-Memory.' *Discourse* 15.2 (Winter 1992–93): 5–37. Print.

LaCapra, Dominick. *Writing History, Writing Trauma.* Baltimore: Johns Hopkins UP, 2001. Print.

Menon, Ritu, and Kamla Bhasin. *Borders & Boundaries: Women in India's Partition.* New Delhi: Kali for Women, 1998. Print.

Moitra, Shefali. *Feminist Thought: Androcentricism, Communication and Objectivity.* Delhi: Munshiram Manoharlal Publishers Pvt. Ltd in association with Centre for Advanced Study in Philosophy, Jadavpur University, Kolkata, 2002. Print.

Mookerjea-Leonard, Debali. 'Disenfranchised Bodies: Jyotirmoyee Devi's Writings on the Partition.' *Gender Online Journal* 38 (2003). Web. 16 Jan. 2014. <http://www.genders.org/g38/g38_leonard.txt>.

Mukherjee, Meenakshi. 'Pawn in the Game.' Review of *The River Churning* by Jyotirmoyee Devi. *The Book Review* 18.12 (1994): 14–15. Print.

Pandey, Gyanendra. *Remembering Partition: Violence, Nationalism, and History in India.* New York: Cambridge UP, 2001. Print.

Radstone, Susannah. 'Social Bonds and Psychical Order: Testimonies.' *Cultural Values* 5: 1 (2001): 59–78. Print.

Spivak, Gayatri Chakravorty. *A Critique of Postcolonial Reason: Toward a History of the Vanishing Present.* Cambridge, Mass.: Harvard UP, 1999. Print.

Sunder Rajan, Rajeswari. *Real and Imagined Women: Gender, Culture and Postcolonialism.* London: Routledge, 1993. Print.

Whitehead, Andrew. 'Cross-channel: *The River Churning*.' Review of *The River Churning* by Jyotirmoyee Devi. *Biblio: A Review of Books* 2: 9 (1996): 19. Print.

In Bangla

Devi, Jyotirmoyee. 'Epar Ganga Opar Ganga.' In *Jyotirmoyee Devir Rachana Sankalan*. Vol. 1. Ed. Subir Raychaudhuri and Abhijit Sen. 1991. Second edition. Kolkata: School of Women's Studies and Dey's Publishing, 2001. 91–189. Print.

———. 'Ahalya Draupadi Tara.' In *Jyotirmoyee Devir Rachana Sankalan*. Vol. 1. Ed. Subir Raychaudhuri and Abhijit Sen. 1991. Second edition. Kolkata: School of Women's Studies and Dey's Publishing, 2001. 221–45. Print.

'The Question is the Story Itself'

Multiplicity of Disnarration in Paul Auster's *The New York Trilogy*

Shinjini Chattopadhyay

According to Peter Brooks, 'narrative desire' is one of the key elements behind the progression of a narrative. 'Desire is always there at the start of a narrative, often in a state of initial arousal, often having reached a state of intensity such that movement must be created, action undertaken, change begun' (Brooks 38). The trajectory of narrative desire is determined to a certain extent by the genre. The phenomenon of postmodernist resistance to grand narratives forces narrative desire to take unconventional routes and consequently the narrative often desists from traversing a unified course and reaching a definitive conclusion. Various works of postmodernist fiction accommodate several narrative lines, which are not distinguished from each other by a hierarchical structure and Gerald Prince terms each of these possible narrative strands as the disnarrated (Prince 303). Prince identifies that indicating 'what could've happened' (Prince 299) is the chief concern of the mode of 'disnarration', the application of which infuses the narrative trajectory with unexplored pathways and hence renders it ambiguous. According to Prince, narrative is a space of certainty and the device of disnarration subverts that very sense of certainty. This moment of subversion is a pivotal point when the narrative departs from the realm of the certain to reach that of the 'otherwise' (302). A particular statement of a character in Paul Auster's *The New York Trilogy* makes this transition seem almost impossible when he says: 'Something happens and then it goes on happening forever. It can never be changed, never be otherwise' (*The New York Trilogy*, 159).

This statement could be considered at best as ironical because the very foundational basis of *The New York Trilogy*, like many other Postmodernist works by Auster, is 'what could've happened.' In his essay, 'The Red Notebook' (190–91), Auster writes that he was inspired by a wrong number to write his first novel, *City of Glass* (1985). An unnamed caller had rung up Auster two days in a row, sometime in the 1980s and had asked for a certain Pinkerton Agency. On both the occasions Auster had hung up after informing the anonymous caller of his mistake. But later he felt that he had 'squandered a rare opportunity' ('The Red Notebook', 190) and tried to make amends for it in his work of fiction. So, in *City of Glass*, Daniel Quinn, the author of detective novels, does not hang up the phone when he is mistaken as a private eye but accepts the opportunity to double up as one and embarks upon a journey to explore the 'otherwise'. Perhaps the best graphical representation of the point of origin of 'disnarration' is found in the graphic novel version of *City of Glass* (53), where Quinn comes across the two identical figures of Peter Stillman and is perplexed about which Stillman to follow. In the figure of Stillman the narrative bifurcates into two possible directions. As soon as Quinn makes a choice and decides to follow one of the Stillmans, abandoning the other, and any choice in this case would have been equally arbitrary, the process of 'disnarration' ensues.

Due to the mode of disnarration, the boundary between factual narrative and fictional narrative in *The New York Trilogy* gets blurred. The realm of fictional narrative is occasionally infiltrated by factual narrative as disparate autobiographical facts about the author are inserted in it. In *City of Glass*, Paul Auster, the author-character, has a son called Daniel, who shares the name of the son of Paul Auster, the actual author (Denes). *Ghosts* begins on 3 February 1947, which is the day Auster was born. Brendan Martin lists the autobiographical elements in *The Locked Room*:

> Fanshawe is an author, and produces a series of poems collected together under the title, *Ground Work*. Fanshawe's sister Ellen is diagnosed as schizophrenic. Paul Auster's own sister named Ellen suffers from mental illness, and Auster himself is the author of a collection of poems and essays entitled *Ground Work*. (Martin 104)

The novel is thus somewhat displaced from the realm of fiction and pushed towards that of autobiographical non-fiction as autobiographical details are interspersed with the fictional narrative. The occasional presence of autobiographical facts destabilises the relationship among the author, narrator and character and thus takes the mode of disnarration further. According to Gérard Genette the dissociation between the author and the narrator is one of the defining features of fictional narrative and the identification of the two agents is characteristic of factual narrative.[1] In *City of Glass*, the boundary between the two types of narrative is rendered ambiguous as what was initially thought to be a third-person narrative suddenly turns out to be a first-person narrative. This sudden change points toward several narrative possibilities which could be best illustrated with the help of the various equation models comprising the author (A), narrator (N) and character (C), conceptualised by Genette (73). In the first instance, if we consider that the first-person narrator, who makes his appearance towards the end of *City of Glass*, is the author, Paul Auster, himself, then we could subscribe to the following formula by Genette and state that since the author (A) is the same as the narrator (N) and the narrator(N) is identified with the narrator–character(C) and the narrator–character(C) in turn is identified with the author(A), the narrative could be termed as an autobiography:

$$A=N=C=A \rightarrow \text{Autobiography (73)}$$

However, identifying the narrative as an autobiography does not immediately mark it as a factual narrative. As Genette mentions, 'nothing prevents the narrator who is duly and deliberately identified with the author . . . from telling a manifestly fictional story' (74). In the case of *City of Glass,* one is unable to locate sufficient historical records to confirm the historical veracity of the events depicted in the narrative, as the plot hardly refers to events outside of its own corpus and related to actual historical occurrences. As a consequence, the narrative is again jettisoned from the certainty of factual autobiography to the realm of fictional uncertainty which opens up various potential threads of disnarration. It is made clear that the unnamed first-person narrator of *City of Glass* is not the same as Daniel Quinn. But the question whether he is Paul Auster, the actual author or just a dissociated first-person narrator, is mired in confusion. If the author is identified with the first-person narrator, then it would resemble the narrative pattern of an autobiography, as previously mentioned. But if the contrary equation is considered then it would open up a plethora of possible narrative patterns which could be made to match several other models of narrative, designed by Genette. Since the identity of the anonymous first-person narrator is never confirmed within the text, it is therefore not possible to unequivocally propound that the narrator–character and the actual author, Paul Auster, are the same. Moreover, the suspicion that the narrator–character and the actual author, Paul Auster, are two different entities, is further strengthened by the similarities in the biographical details between Paul Auster, the author-character, and Paul Auster, the actual author. Thus the new equation, that becomes possible considering this situation, is that the actual author (A), Paul Auster, is not the same as the first-person narrator (N); the first-person narrator(N) and the narrator–character(C) are the same but the narrator–character(C) is not identified with the actual author (A), Paul Auster. Following Genette's model, this new formation of the narrative could be termed as 'homodiegetic fiction'.

A≠N=C≠A→homodiegetic fiction (73).

This formation would immediately lead to the question that if the first person narrator is not Paul Auster, the actual author, then who is the actual author and if the actual author is at all present in the narrative. The presence in the text of Paul Auster, the author-character, renders it difficult to definitively establish that the actual author, Paul Auster, is absent from the text. The biographical link reduces the possibility of regarding the author–character as completely detached from the actual author and of placing the author–character purely within the space of fiction. However, the text confirms that the first-person narrator is a friend of Paul Auster, the author-character, and hence not the same as him. Therefore, if we consider that Paul Auster, the author-character, is the same as Paul Auster, the actual author, then the following narrative design emerges: the actual author Paul Auster (A) is not the same as the first-person narrator (N), the first-person narrator (N) is not the same as Paul Auster, the author–character (C) but Paul Auster, the author–character (C), is the same as Paul Auster, the actual author (A). According to Genette, this is the narrative pattern of a third person autobiography.

A≠N≠C=A→ third person autobiography (Genette 73)

However, since the text does not explicitly mention that Paul Auster, the author–character, and Paul Auster, the actual author, are the same, the alternative possibility that the two of them are two distinctly separate homonymous entities should also be taken into account. The alternative possibility would lead to the formation of yet another narrative pattern, where Paul Auster, the actual author (A), is not the same as the first-person narrator (N); the first person narrator is not the same as Paul Auster, the author–character (C) and Paul Auster, the author–character (C), is not the same as Paul Auster, the actual author (A). According to Genette, this is the narrative design of a heterodiegetic fiction.

A≠N≠C≠A→ heterodiegetic fiction (Genette 73)

Thus Auster's mode of disnarration accommodates the narrative patterns of the autobiography, homodiegetic fiction, heterodiegetic fiction and the third-person autobiography within the same narrative plane and the lack of definitive assertions about the figures of the author, narrator and character makes each of these patterns equally suitable for the narrative and locates it in a perpetual state of the 'otherwise', that of disnarration.

One of the principal functions of a detective in fiction is to collect disparate evidence, arrange them in such a way that a logical coherence would emerge out of a group of disjointed details and then follow the logical progression which would ultimately lead him to the person responsible for the act of crime in question. Therefore a largely objective process of reading the evidence becomes instrumental in the course of unmasking the guilty, where the detective tries to refrain from imposing his own interpretations as much as possible. In this essential process of analysing the evidence, the detective is joined by the reader. The reader reads the clues alongside the detective as the investigation progresses. In *Ghosts*, the second story of *The New York Trilogy*, Auster describes such an ideal objective process of investigation:

> In every report he has written so far, action holds forth over interpretation. For example: The subject walked from Columbus Circle to Carnegie Hall. No references to the weather, no mention of the traffic, no stab at trying to guess what the subject might

> be thinking. The report confines itself to known and verifiable facts, and beyond this limit it does not try to go. (144)

However, contrary to this proclamation, the detectives in *The New York Trilogy* do not limit themselves to an objective reading of the circumstances and are always interested in 'what could've happened'. While reading the narrative made available to them by their respective subjects of investigation, the detectives expand the scope of the narrative by weaving in their own interpretations. In *City of Glass*, Quinn tracks every movement of Peter Stillman Sr. for several days and is unable to make any sense of it. He asserts that there are only two possibilities in the case of Stillman: 'Either Stillman knew what he was doing or he didn't' (*The New York Trilogy*, 61). Quinn prefers to believe in the first option because according to the detective stories he is familiar with, the investigation of the detective always yields some form of meaning. Therefore, instead of dismissing Stillman's activities as aimless ramblings, he reads a pattern into it. He constructs a map from his exhaustive notes in which he had recorded every footstep of Stillman and sees that the path traversed by Stillman everyday, spells a particular alphabet, the sum of which Quinn anticipates to be the phrase, 'The Tower of Babel'. In *Ghosts*, the detective Blue searches for some purpose in the activities of his respective subject of investigation, Mr Black. He reflects on the possible directions the narrative could take:

> . . . he discovers that making up stories could be a pleasure in itself. He thinks that perhaps White and Black are brothers and that a large sum of money is at stake . . . Still another story has it that White is a renegade agent from the FBI . . . and has struck out on his own to conduct some peripheral investigation not necessarily sanctioned by his superiors. (*The New York Trilogy*, 141)

Thus the detective-reader not only carries out an objective investigation of the circumstances, but is engaged in constantly anticipating the future course of events. Their innovative interpretation of the events and predictions about the future trajectory of the same adds to the multifariousness of the narrative and points towards the possible directions the narrative could have taken.

The desired end of a detective novel is unmasking the culprit or solving the mystery. The three stories in *The New York Trilogy* initially operate within the conventions of detective fiction but as the narrative progresses, they keep resisting the discovery of a definitive answer to the mysteries and reveal the potential incapacity of fictional modes of mystery detection. Consequently, they go beyond the circumscription of the genre of crime fiction. In *City of Glass,* Quinn hopes to compensate for his lack of experience in the field of actual detective work by reading fictional accounts from which he gains certain preconceived notions about mystery detection and tries to interpret the situation under inspection according to those predetermined conditions instead of observing the spontaneous flow of events. In *Ghosts* also the real-life private eye Black points out the existing lacuna between fictional detective work and being a detective in real life when he says, 'real-life detective work can be pretty dull' (*The New York Trilogy*, 177). The narrative flow of a conventional detective fiction gradually brings the readers closer to the culprit and ends with unmasking his/her true identity. On the contrary, in *The New York Trilogy* the sheer existence of the subjects of investigation for Quinn, Mr Blue and the first-person narrator in *The Locked Room* becomes increasingly volatile. The Stillmans disappear all of a sudden, Blue finds out that the person he was supposed to follow was in turn assigned to follow him and Fanshawe does not come out of the locked room and thereby never confirms his true identity. Unlike the usual conclusion of a detective story all that remains at the end of these three stories is a sense of ambiguity, an unresolved enigma. The narrative of crime fiction is supremely dominated by the idea of attaining the truth. But the genre is made to disintegrate as the mode of disnarration in *The New York Trilogy* relentlessly asserts: 'You can't possibly know what's true or not true. You'll never know' (*The New York Trilogy*, 306).

In *The New York Trilogy*, much as the genre, Auster experiments with characters by adding multiple dimensions to their identity, which indicate towards various narrative possibilities under the scanner of disnarration. To begin with, Quinn lives in a 'triad of selves' (6). Under the pseudonym William Wilson, Quinn writes stories of the adventures of Max Work, a fictional private eye.

Max Work gradually becomes an integral part of Quinn's life, 'his interior brother, his comrade in solitude' (*The New York Trilogy*, 6). At a certain point, Work's presence becomes so overpowering that Quinn tries to go beyond his identity of an author of crime fiction and becomes a real-life detective. But the act of assuming an identity that is not his own infuses an element of indeterminacy in Quinn's self from which he never really recovers. He can never successfully grow out of his identity of a writer and continues weaving out his own narrative from the results of his investigation.[2] In *The Locked Room* the first-person narrator and Fanshawe are shown to be sharing a very intimate bond since childhood. But when the narrator takes up Fanshawe's vacant position in his family and makes Fanshawe's wife his own, the absent Fanshawe becomes a threat to the narrator. The narrator realises that every atom of his existence is attached to that of Fanshawe and he fears that he might have lost his autonomous existence. He is threatened by the possibility that his identity might eventually become inseparable from that of Fanshawe and what he has been considering so far as the narrative of his own life might actually be that of Fanshawe's. A similar crisis of identity is faced by Blue and Black in *Ghosts* as well. After realising that they are mirror images of each other, each of them attempts to establish his supremacy of self over the other, notwithstanding that their individual existence is dependent on the simultaneous existence of the other. As Black says of Blue, 'he needs my eyes looking at him. He needs me to prove he is alive' (*The New York Trilogy*, 178). Black and Blue could be regarded as two possible narrative directions: the narration and the disnarration. Since one validates the other, as soon as one of them is obliterated, the other ceases to exist as well. So when Blue beats Black to death he puts an end to one of the strands of the narrative. In such a situation, Blue also cannot operate autonomously because he does not have the validation of the other narrative. Hence the story cannot advance and 'from this moment on, we know nothing' (*The New York Trilogy,* 192).

When the three stories are juxtaposed against one another, we see the same pattern emerging again and again which is the account of a particular character embarking on a quest to find his double or adversary and in the process encountering the experiences of confinement and facing a threat to his identity. The authorial persona of Paul Auster speaks through the narrator of *The Locked Room* and confirms that '[T]hese three stories are finally the same story, but each one represents a different stage in my awareness of what it is about' (*The New York Trilogy,* 288).

Thus each story indicates what could have happened and is the disnarration of the other two. If one attempts to draw a blueprint of the narrative structure of *The New York Trilogy* it would perhaps be something like a spiral where each narrative strand is connected to the other and is spiralling outwards, thus nesting inside itself further strands of narrative. In the movie, *The Inner Life of Martin Frost* (2007) directed by Auster himself, a graphical representation of such a spiral figure is shown. In his very first novel, Auster draws out the narrative blueprint which is to function as the foundational basis of many of his subsequent works. In this narrative structure, story and plot are intermingled and it is difficult to identify the author, the character and the narrator separately. The only element that has a distinct presence is the narrative progression, which can take any possible direction between that of narration and of disnarration.

Notes

1. 'The relation between author and narrator remains to be considered. It seems to me that their rigorous identification (*A* = N), insofar as it can be established, defines factual narrative, in which, in Searle's terms, the author assumes full responsibility for the assertions of his narrative, and consequently grants no shred of autonomy to any narrator whatsoever. Conversely, their dissociation (*A* ¥ = N) defines fiction, that is, a type of narrative whose veracity is not seriously assumed by the author' (Genette 70).
2. If we apply Genette's equation model of narratives to the situation of Daniel Quinn and Max Work, we would come across a very interesting pattern. Since Quinn confesses that he has interiorised the persona of Max Work within his real self, to the extent that he tries to emulate the fictional character in real life, we might assume that he introduces certain autobiographical elements in the character of Max Work. Following this assumption we would obtain the narrative design of a third person autobiography where

Daniel Quinn (A) is not the same as the third person narrator (N) of his works; the narrator is not the same as the character Max Work (C); however, Max Work (C) is the same as Daniel Quinn (A). A≠N≠C=A→third person autobiography (Genette 73).

WORKS CITED

Auster, Paul. 'The Red Notebook.' *Collected Prose*. New York: Faber and Faber, 2003. 176–91. Print.

———. *City of Glass*. Script adapt. Paul Karasik and David Mazzucchelli. Illus. David Mazzucchelli. New York: Avon Books, 1994. Print.

———, dir. *The Inner Life of Martin Frost*. Peter Newman Productions, 2007. Film.

———. *The New York Trilogy*. New York: Penguin Books, 1988. Print.

Brooks, Peter. *Reading for the Plot: Design and Intention in Narrative*. Cambridge: Harvard UP, 1992. Print.

Denes, Melissa. 'The Dark Side of Happiness.' Web. 30 November 2013. http://www.theguardian.com/world/2006/feb/04/gender.books.

Genette, Gérard. *Fiction and Diction*. Trans. Catherine Porter. London: Cornell UP, 1993. Print.

Martin, Brendan. *Paul Auster's Postmodernity*. New York: Routledge, 2008. Print.

Prince, Gerald. 'The Disnarrated.' *Narrative Theory: Critical Concepts in Literary and Cultural Studies*. Vol 1. Ed. Mieke Bal. London: Routledge, 2004. 297–305. Print.

The Politics of Disnarration

Nation and Narrative in *The Storyteller*

Sreya Dutt

The aim of this paper is to establish the 'disnarration' of marginal communities from the national mainstream through a close reading of *The Storyteller*. The erasure or effacing of marginal communities such as the Machiguenga needs to be seen in terms of the incapacity or narrowness of national discourse itself. Co-existent with the process of past 'disnarration' in terms of the conscious negation of a community with the application of violence, is the attempt on the part of nationalist structures in the present to subsume such communal identities within their fold. Thus the preservation and the iteration of the identities of such peripheral communities may be rendered possible through a process associated with the political polemics of 'disnarration' on their part as well. This stance may be viewed with respect to an attitude of resistance and subversion (on the part of the community) towards hegemonic national frameworks and their coercive and conformism-inducing drives.

In *The Storyteller,* Mario Vargas Llosa presents the journey of a narrator who seeks to uncover the silence surrounding a particular indigenous community in Peru, the Machiguenga. The Machiguenga are a tribe of people who live a nomadic life wandering through the Urubamba river valley in South-eastern Peru. This journey also coincides with his search for his own long-lost friend Saúl Zuratas. Written in 1987, Vargas Llosa's *The Storyteller* seems to deal with the issue of representation in far greater depth than other narratives of the time and from several angles, weaving in several different strands of narrative textures. For the narrator, an academic and intellectual modelled after the author Vargas Llosa himself, the Machiguenga community is the subject of a lifelong passion and intense fascination. In fact the narrator's life can be seen as a mapping of that abiding interest and its development. In his quest for a deeper search of their ways of life he is seen to arrive upon a series of stunning realisations.

The arresting figure of Saúl Zuratas or *Mascarita*[1] revealed to be the *hablador*[2] at the very end is the crux of the issue of representation. *Mascarita* is an incredible figure whose active engagement with the Machiguenga tribe in the heart of Amazonia leads him to become one of them. He is indeed a projection of the deepest desires of the narrator himself, whose wish to unravel the mystery of the *hablador* figure can never be fulfilled as the Machiguengas themselves remain silent on the subject.

In *The Storyteller,* Saul Zuratas, the son of a Jewish immigrant is alienated from the society he is born into, due to a birth mark which renders his appearance as strange and subject to ridicule. It is this birth mark that earns him the name *Mascarita.* The story traces *Mascarita's* journey of self-discovery as he assimilates himself into the Machiguenga community and becomes their storyteller. The role of the storyteller is particularly important in the case of a wandering people like the Machiguengas. The storyteller keeps the Machiguenga belief system and myths alive by taking his stories to their isolated settlements scattered sporadically across the Amazonian rainforests of Peru. Though forced to feel alienated by the dominant white society of Lima, *Mascarita's* white racial background does not prevent him from being completely accepted by the Machiguenga community. Acknowledging him as one of their own, they grant him the position of the *hablador* because of his deep and abiding interest in their myths and beliefs. Although *Mascarita* is the central protagonist in this narrative, the story is told from the perspective of a fellow-student of Saul, the narrator, who is deeply intrigued by the *hablador* figure in Machiguenga society. The narrator's voice alternates with the stories of the *hablador* as he journeys to different settlements and meets various figures. The *hablador* must constantly be on the move – perhaps reflecting the dynamic nature of the Machiguenga myth systems and the wandering lifestyle of the community, the key to their survival in the face of adversity, be it from the conquering Incas or the 'Tree-tappers' during the horrors of the 'rubber boom'. This wandering, nomadic lifestyle is touted to be the reason behind their survival from variegated, hostile, life-threatening forces.

The figure of the *hablador* appears to be almost a taboo that the narrator is compelled to encounter. His persistent questioning of the Machiguengas, twenty-five odd years after his visit to the interior of Amazonia, shows them to be part of an ongoing process of integration within the fold of the modern nation-state of Peru, thanks to the efforts of earnest and zealous missionaries and anthropologists. The community continues, however, to inhabit isolated pockets of the Amazonian forest. The narrator is seen to visit two remote but permanent Machiguenga settlements in the Amazon namely 'Nueva Mundo'[3] and 'Nueva Luz'[4] with a television crew to document the lives of this elusive and mysterious community. The Machiguengas perform their identity for the television crew – they sing, dance and are even willing to explain the community's rituals and customs. What is most poignant is that they insist on singing the Peruvian national anthem – is it an act of irony, of showcasing their 'integration' within the nation? Is it a performance of thanks to be witnessed by all of Peru for the state's dictum of 'ordering' their lives into a settled existence from the erstwhile nomadic way of life?

The narrator re-imagines and reconstructs the Machiguenga myths and stories of creation, right down to the 'rubber boom', the arrival of the White Man and the tribe's subsequent widespread detention, persecution and slaughter. This reveals a dynamic and living heritage of myth as opposed to the static communities in 'Nueva Mundo' and 'Nueva Luz' who seem to mechanically perform or showcase their indigenous identity. To imagine this throbbing and vibrant world of tradition under flux there is a constant re-working and re-telling of myth on the part of the narrator, which is supplemented by the *hablador*'s tales of travel, also re-constituted by narratorial imagination. Interestingly, the narrator is denied first-hand access to this living tradition of myth that is borne in the person of the *hablador*. The *hablador* is the carrier of this tradition of story-telling, linking its various members by the common thread of myth-making that encapsulates what is probably the most active and essential component of the Machiguenga culture.

The issue of representing a small and marginal tribe living in the deepest interior of the country with sensitivity would always be a complex and problematic literary enterprise. Vargas Llosa is well aware of his predecessors, the *indigenista*[5] novelists and the indigenists of the historical past who fell into the trap of essentialism. The 'noble savage' trope oft used and abused in fiction can find no room in a work as rich and nuanced as Vargas Llosa's. To gain a full understanding of the inner workings of the Machiguenga way of life, the outsider to their culture and belief systems must become *one* of them – only then will access be granted to their inner world as illustrated through the *hablador, Mascarita*. The process of complete transformation on his part can never be fully explained but it stems from *Mascarita*'s deep interest in the Machiguenga people. It is also driven by his active desire to know them and also the tribe's unquestioning acceptance of him despite his facial deformity that has scarred him for life.

It is all speculation on the part of the narrator with respect to how *Mascarita* is accorded acceptance and recognition by the Machiguenga community, and *Mascarita*'s story of integration remains shrouded in mystery as does the *hablador* figure himself. The purported conversations that *Mascarita* carries out with his parrot and also with 'Tasurinchi', a resident deity of Machiguenga folklore too are imaginatively reconstructed by the narrator. As readers, we can never access the mind of the *hablador* directly, our entry to the inner workings of his mind is twice removed as he can be approached only through narratorial rendering. This point may be seen in the light of 'narration' and 'disnarration' as opposing forces which govern the portrayal of the *hablador* figure himself. The *hablador* does not wish to be witnessed by anyone outside the Machiguenga community, let alone narrated. To illustrate this, we are shown the death of the photographer in the beginning of the novel who managed to take a photograph of him and displayed it in an exhibition in Italy. There is also the incident of Mr Schnell, the anthropologist being seized with a debilitating fever due to his presence during one of the *hablador*'s storytelling sessions. Contesting the drive of the *hablador* to remain outside the purview of Western, rationalist and empirical paradigms of documenting the Machinguengas, is the personal impetus of the narrator to unlock the cipher that the *hablador* insists on remaining. Narrating the *hablador*, however much it remains in the realm of surmise and conjecture for the narrator is what defines the latter – the desire to know. The limits of knowledge itself remain sharply defined with respect to a project that is almost delusional on the part of the narrator: to seek out a resisting, elusive and even deeply hostile figure.

Vargas Llosa seems to be charting three agents of possible representation: firstly, the narrator. The narrator can only gain the degree and depth of knowledge he does through the painstaking accumulation and archiving of data undertaken as a lifetime's enterprise by dedicated and methodical social scientists like the Schnells, and the work of missionaries usually patronising and deeply prejudiced in their stance. The Schnells and missionaries may be said to belong to a second order of narrators. It is *Mascarita*, who becomes a Machiguenga himself, who is the ultimate narrator with the most immediate and intimate access to the Machiguenga. The Machiguenga story is told through *Mascarita*, who does not speak directly but is re-created through the narrator's imagination and also by a detailed and exhaustive study of extensive material related to the tribe. The novel emerges out of a joint collaboration of research and a deep level of affect and emotional identification on the part of the narrator in the light of his personal affinity and interest in the *hablador*, going back to their days as colleagues in the University of Lima.

Perhaps it would not be too far-fetched to suggest that the narrator figure and the author Mario Vargas Llosa himself form a blurred identity – Vargas Llosa is, after a fashion, a *hablador* himself, and his attempt to search for alternative and inventive channels of representation of the Latin American reality(s), one of the key areas of concern of Boom literature, finds expression thus.

There is little confluence of opinion regarding the publication which may be regarded as the 'beginning' of this explosion of Latin American writing that stylistically and formally challenged the genre of the novel in terms of such epic proportions. Critics like John King have made references (75) to Carlos Fuentes' *La región más transparante* (*Where the Air is Clear*), published in the 1940s and Mario Vargas Llosa's *La Ciudad y los Perros* (*The Imposters*) of the '50's which won the Biblioteca Breve prize. The publication of Julio Cortazar's *Rayuela* or *Hopscotch* in 1963 is also regarded to be a major event in the Boom. The Boom coincided with the Cuban Revolution which was invested in the hope of, among other things, the recognition of a uniquely Latin American aesthetics and artistic sensibility, and the need to give credence to the contingencies and specificities of the lived realities of Latin America. Cuba invited young writers to the country, published their work in the magazine *Casas de las Ámerica*[6] and initiated literary symposiums and conferences. The Boom would be both formally innovative and rooted in a uniquely Latin American experience.

Vargas Llosa's narrator is engaged in a 'telling' of alternate histories of communities forgotten and yet also attempted to be incorporated within the nation-state by the rather artificial and contrived apparatus of the state itself. Alternate histories are indicative of the Boom's quest, as a literary movement, to highlight and foreground uniquely Latin American realities vis-à-vis deeply entrenched structures of exploitation and denial that indigenous communities were subject to.[7] Mario Vargas Llosa takes the process of representation a step further in a refreshingly different direction – he re-creates the Machiguenga way of life, mythologies and histories from an insider's point of view in a novel that reveals much more than years of archival work could ever have hoped to.

The Storyteller showcases several different ways of cultural interactions and through them points out the difficulty in prioritising any one form as superior to others. The novel also illustrates that there can be no one definitive path to cultural understanding. *Mascarita's* method of cultural assimilation into the Machiguenga cultural milieu calls for complete eradication of his white urban roots. For him, aspiring to integrate into the Machiguenga society implies a total immersion into the Machiguenga cultural order. He strongly disapproves of any anthropological or ethnological probing into their cultural beliefs. He looks upon the activities of anthropologists as immoral and sees them as perpetrating violence against the tribes, which he feels will lead to their subsequent obliteration. The Schnells and the Summer Institute of Linguistics represent this latter form of cultural interaction, which threatens the very fabric of Machiguenga society through academic zealousness. The prime objective of the Institute and the Schnells was to have the Machiguenga community lead a settled existence and this aim is realised in the form of two settlements – 'New World' and 'New Light'. The very names carry in them an echo of the colonial past. They are taught to sing the Peruvian national anthem in Machiguenga, read the Bible translated into their language and appoint *cacique*[8] figures within their community. The Machiguenga society was characterised by the absence of a central authoritative figure. The very appointment of a *cacique* is thus an aberration against the Machiguenga social structure.

The narrator of the *The Storyteller* may be viewed as a strange means through which two concurrent stories are iterated. One strand of the narrative relates the story of the narrator's own professional life and the course of his friendship with Saúl Zuratas. This narrative alternates with glimpses of Machiguenga cosmogony and myth. The complexity of the text lies not only in this dual narrative focus. More fraught than the seeming incompatability of the narratives is the ethical orientation framing each literary strain. The narrator, as the master of the narrative, owns its language in many respects. This is because only he can *render* the events and happenings associated with the *hablador*. He processes the vast body of documentary research material that the Schnells have collected, and reconstructs it with respect to the *hablador*'s journeys and the re-creation of Machiguenga myth. Yet this sense of ownership is undermined largely by the completely foreign nature of the Machiguenga language and culture that he is not acquainted with. To possess words to such a degree that they can be recorded within written signs shows a certain degree of assimilation in a cultural master narrative. To record a culture as one's own implies the placement of the writer as a participant in the culture.

This is the manner in which the narrator of *The Storyteller* is situated. He can record the words of another culture only through translation or through the appropriation of an imagined language, only by somehow bringing these words into his own literary vision. However, there is no complete ownership of language here. By trying to reconstitute the Machiguenga story, as related by an elusive and amorphous *hablador*, projected or imagined in the figure of Saúl Zuratas, the narrator creates a device to control what is largely an uncontrollable narrative. He imagines the Machiguenga and their rituals of storytelling, and only by the projection of these tales as filters of his cultural assumptions can a semi-linear narrative emerge which will bear coherence for Western or 'rational' readers. The evocation of the mystery figure of the *hablador* also serves to satisfy the narrator's desire to know in writing a tribe that has remained a cryptic puzzle for him. Yet by invoking the Zuratas figure to tell his story, the narrator's primary conflict emerges. Both the oral and the written discourses are engaged in a struggle of each retaining its own autonomy. Tension remains between the oral and written, narration and disnarration. This refers to the oral heritage of the Machiguengas as having been accessed through secondary sources via a body of anthropological work and subsequently written by agents external to the community in the form of scientists and missionaries. The elusive community and their mysterious *hablador* can only be accessed through writing that has been negotiated through a number of sources and remains well-removed from the native epistemology of the community itself. Significant absences and slippages emerge in the ensuing face-off between oral and written which prove that the issue of representation and the narratability of the Machiguenga is itself a deeply problematic area.

The text traces the attempt of the narrator to write about his college friend, Saúl Zuratas and an indigenous community he has never been quite able to possess mentally. As Sara Castro-Klarén has argued (142), there is always something that is just tantalisingly beyond the reach of the narrator. He cannot envision a totality, and thereby creates an imagined account of Machiguenga rituals and cosmogony, that which cannot be narrated, being unutterable, and yet which he cannot allow to remain unnarrated.

The Storyteller consists of three embedded narratives, each serving as a gateway to the next, governed apparently by the figure of Saúl Zuratas who acts as conduit framing and carrying all three narratives, but is really controlled by Vargas Llosa's desire to posses the Machiguenga on a mental level. These narratives form three 'diagetic levels' as theorised by Julianne Newmark. The first is the level of the narrator, the second the level of *Mascarita* and the stories of the *hablador*s which he has inherited, and the third level is the *hablador*s' stories. The *Mascarita*/Zuratas figure presented to the reader is the creation of the narrator, who is, of course, a creation of Vargas Llosa himself.

To willingly occupy the social position that Saul Zuratas does, calls for great courage and deep conviction, and his choices will always be regarded as aberrant, and at times, even verging on madness. Narratives such as *The Storyteller* play a decisive role in making dominant social groups aware of social inequities that are taken for granted to the extent of being rendered invisible. The dominant discourse deliberately makes it so. Cultural understanding may at times seem implausible or impossible, but the first step towards greater cultural communication can only come about through the acknowledgment of the existence of cultural barriers.

Notes

1. '*Mascarita*' meaning 'the masked one' in Spanish
2. 'Hablador' meaning 'storyteller', or simply, 'one who speaks, narrates or recounts'. The term originates from the Spanish verb 'hablar' which means 'to speak'. The original Spanish title of the novel is 'El Hablador' which has been translated into English as 'The Storyteller.'
3. 'Nueva Mundo' or 'New World' in Spanish
4. 'Nueva Luz' or 'New Light" in Spanish
5. This was a political and aesthetic movement that developed in Mexico and the Andean countries in the early twentieth century which consisted of largely stereotypical and uni-dimensional portrayals of indigenous peoples without any subjective rendering of their lived realities. This literary movement took no cognisance whatsoever of the histories of brutal oppression, systematic persecution and subsequent erasure that indigenous communities were subject to across Latin America since the arrival of Spanish colonisers.
6. A prestigious literary magazine published in Cuba which showcased the most radical, politically charged and stylistically inventive work coming out of Latin America.
7. For a poignant, lyrical and yet deeply informative account of the history of colonisation and neo-colonisation in Latin America, see

Open Veins of Latin America by the Uruguayan historian Eduardo Galeano.

8. The 'cacique' refers to rural landlords who originated in the aftermath of the disorder and chaos of the Mexican revolution and were characterised by their brutally oppressive and tyrannical administration.

WORKS CITED

Castro Klarén, Sara. 'Understanding Mario Vargas Llosa.' *Chasqui* 20 (1991): 141–43. *JSTOR*. Web. 20 Jan. 2013.

Galeano, Eduardo. *The Open Veins of Latin America*. Trans. Cedric Belfrage. New York: Monthly Review Press, 1973.

King, John. 'The Boom of the Latin American Novel.' *The Cambridge Companion to the Latin American Novel*. Ed. Efraín Kristal. Cambridge: University Press, 2006. 75–81. Print.

Newmark, Julianne. 'Language, Absence and Narrative Impossibility in Mario Vargas Llosa's *El Hablador*.' *Latin American Literary Review* 31 (2003): 5–22. JSTOR. Web. 24 Jan. 2013.

Vargas Llosa, Mario. *The Storyteller*. Trans. Helen Lane. New York: Farrar, Strauss and Giroux, 1987. Print.

Historical Fiction, Disnarrated and the Communal Stratagem

Questioning the Counterfactual Constructions of History in Bankimcandra Chatterji's *Anandamath* and Kanaiyalal Maneklal Munshi's *Jay Somanatha*

Rohit Dutta Roy

The disnarrated, writes Prince, 'covers all the events that do not happen though they could have and are nonetheless referred to (in a negative or hypothetical mode) by the narrative text. It can refer to the future, the present or the past. It frequently consists of hopes, desires, imaginings and ponderings, unreasonable expectations and incorrect beliefs' (*Narrative as Theme,* 30). Referring to Coste, he would reiterate that one should conceive of narrated action as 'the presence as opposed to the absence of alternative courses of action for the narrative participants' ('Revisiting Narrativity', 30). In my paper I will be emphasising the ability of a linguistic form to invoke contextual and associated meanings. In doing this I will be focussing on Ryan's functional delineation of the virtual narrative which is less dependent on linguistic manifestation but is most often implicit or inferred by the reader (Ryan, *Narrative as Virtual Reality*). As a sub-category of disnarration, it belongs to the level of plot development and can be seen as unrealised or unrealisable plot versions.

I will be analysing this through two texts – Bankimcandra Chatterji's *Anandamath* and Kanaiyalal Maneklal Munshi's *Jay Somanatha*. Placing this within the broader context of disnarration, the disnarrated may be defined as counterfactual, what could have happened but didn't, and as such it is part of the course of the plot events. Or should we say the alternative plot events?

Even though the primary focus of studies in disnarration may have hinged on 'narrating', the thrust area of my research remains the narrated. The disnarrated therefore, has come to include counterfactuals, often articulated in a hypothetical mode where the real may not be discernible from the imagined. And yet the events within the textual plane narrated in the realistic model of actual events and occurrences, falling in the category of alternate histories, have often been kept out of the pale of the disnarrated, primarily due to the very ordering of counterfactual events being posited as actual events within the ontological hierarchy of the narrative world (Dannenberg 116). The disnarrated is a part of the fabula, which together is based on the syuzhet or the plot and has no independent existence without their narrative realisation (Meister 16).

While the historical narrative is based on documentary evidence, the fictional narrative or the plot as conceived by the author posits its own fabula as its basis and presents itself, often rearranged, in the manner of a discourse. This, in the Indian situation, I would argue, presents a case for the counterfactual and the disnarrated coming closer. Given that, people who envisioned themselves as historical chroniclers, took to literature to attain greater credibility and envision a role of historical reworking in the realm of popular memory; while the litterateurs dabbled in history, reformulating it. This becomes all the more problematic when one realises the conscious attempt to reconstruct the past based on contemporary needs, under the compulsions of a colonial rule, and how it led to the birth of false historiographical traditions.

To discuss how the literary project led to the pervasiveness of the colonial historic–religious constructs, its popularisation amongst the general readers through translations in the vernaculars and growing commodisation of literary texts, is beyond the purview of this paper. However, what one can safely affirm is that narratives having elements of counterfactuals and what Prince many years later would characterise as disnarrated, had immense effect on the collective memorialisation and amnesia that communalism invokes.

According to Prince, something is disnarrated 'only if it designates in that diegesis a possibility that remains unrealized' (*Narrative as Theme,* 34). In both the texts studied here the possibility of a community (whom Chatterji and Munshi both consider the rightful inhabitants of a sacred land) reclaiming what was rightfully theirs, and avenging the grave injustice, serve as the topoi. *Anandamath* ends in an anti-climax, the Healer convincing Satyananda that their motherland would benefit from the English rule which has been ushered in after having wiped out the Muslim rule, an act which in itself contained the seeds of Hindu rule in the foreseeable future. Munshi's narrative too ends with a note of possibility with the plundered Somanatha standing tall, prayers being offered from its ramparts and Chaula's death linking a union with her deity, perhaps suggesting a sense of communal unity.

Prince carefully dissects narrative categories to distinguish the disnarrated from the unnarratable and the unnarrated and to link it with authorial statements, character's vision, the domains of description and argumentation, narrative rhythm, and characterisation devices (*Narrative as Theme*). The disnarrated is defined as 'all those passages in a text that consider what did not or does not happen but could have happened' (*Narrative as Theme*, 34). The disnarrated, therefore, emerges as a kind of negative, or hypothetical, narrative mode.

The disnarrated if used in narrating is focused on the realities of representation as opposed to the representation of realities, and plays a larger role than the normative (Prince, 'The Disnarrated', 1). Negatives and the disnarrated therefore serve ethical and political ends. They direct the readers' attention to the discursive context of the text, working with the readers' decoding practices embedded as they are in their sociocultural matrix, urging them to read metonymically (Karttunen 439). Perhaps it is in this context that counterfactuals in the mode of disnarration leave little room for subverting dominant reading strategies. At times determining the discursive space, or even without doing so, they do concretise the conceptual framework, semiotic structures and manners of relating through identity practices. Negatives do not record a neutrally observable reality but narrate in the manner of what is expected in a given situation and of a particular person, or perhaps a religious community.

Harking back to Prince, in the context of both *Jay Somanatha* and *Anandamath*, the function of the disnarrated is a rhetorical or an interpretive one. It foregrounds ways of creating a situation or ordering an experience. The narrator in both instances fantasises about how things could have gone, might have gone, but being historical fiction this propensity guides the entire novel, presenting not fact but wish. The reorganisation of events that gives the disnarrated its negative potential is then at work throughout. How then does disnarration contribute to a theory of counterfactuals in historical fiction or vice versa? 'A counterfactual involves a clear contrasting relationship between a factual sequence of events and a counterfactual proposition that changes the factual by creating a new antecedent and an altered outcome' (Dannenberg 130).

This study focuses on how the disnarrated contributes to the development of a theme. My concern is also about the reaction that these texts try to evoke in the minds of a homogenised Hindu consciousness and how the reader receives texts with a narrative of negation, also a form of the disnarrated. Therefore, from the textual plane, the disnarrated can be analysed through modes of reception which order a set of discursive reactions, ranging from antagonism to revivalism, in order to tap into the militaristic potential of a homogenised community suddenly guided by a cohesive force due to the potential of the narrative.

Whether it is the scene where Gangasarvajna, the priest of the Somanatha temple stands between the holy lingam and the invaders in *Jay Somanatha* or Satyananda's meeting with the Healer who implores him to see reason, to give up the hope of liberation of the motherland and welcome the British rule even as Satyananda's Anandamath falls apart, these are a few specific instances of disnarration. Yet this study is based on the tenor on which the entire novel is written by both the authors. If Chatterji's target reader, to borrow the concept from Benedict Anderson, is the imagined community of resurgent Hindus, by 1937 when K. M. Munshi wrote his *Jay Somanatha*, the ground realities would have suggested that Chatterji's vision of the Santans was coming true, with the aggressive Hindutva politics that started organising itself in the 1920s on an exclusively and explicitly anti-Muslim platform.

The dreadful famine of 1770 in which one-third of Bengal's population had perished forms the background of *Anandamath*.

Chatterji would collect much of his source material from William Wilson Hunter's *Annals of Rural Bengal.* The first part of the novel ends with a general account of the rampage of the Santan army, mostly against Muslims, and its eventual defeat by British forces. The novel draws to a close with the interpolation of the Healer, who not only implores Satyananda to give up the hope of liberation of the motherland and surrender to the British army, but also tells him that this is providential and that the Hindus need a benefactor to attain modern prowess. Therefore while the Santans do overthrow the 'Muslim' Nawab, until then indirectly controlled by the British, they fail to do much beyond that and this results in bringing Bengal under direct colonial control.

Based on the Sanyasi and Fakir rebellion, which rocked northern Bengal and adjacent areas of Bihar between 1763 and 1800, Chatterji's narrative valorises the Dasnami Sanyasis while the erasure of the contribution of the Madari Fakirs towards the same provides us with the objectives of our study. One needs to read the silences in the text to understand its underlying propaganda. Not only does Chatterji refer to the Muslims with contempt during the course of the narrative but also replaces many of the references to the English with those to Muslims, to subdue the militant tone of the novel. In the process he not only undermines the philosophical affinities between the two religious orders but also chooses to remain silent on their mutual relationship, organisational network and communication with the followers.

The Sanyasis, known for their martial tradition, were involved in landholding, money-lending and trade in raw silk, piece goods, broad cloth, copper and spices (Bandyopadhyay 161). Affected as they were by the Company's high revenue demands, resumption of rent-free tenures and commercial monopoly, their understanding of colonial rule shaped their concept of resistance (Bandyopadhyay 161). Their ranks had swelled with the survivors of the famine of 1769–70, a large number of aggrieved small zamindars, disbanded soldiers and the rural poor joining their ranks (Bandyopadhyay 161). Chatterji would change the details of much of this to transform the rebellion into a battle or a confrontational war organised by a clandestine organisation against the British. Therefore, the Saiva sanyasis who were illiterate in real life, become the militant educated Vaishnava Santans and he paints them as an anti-colonial cohesive rebel outfit (Das, *The Artist in Chains,* 154). His personal interest in the activities of secret societies from his own readings in Italian history as well as contemporary materials from the exploits of Vasudev Balwant Phadke informs the narrative (Das, *A History of Indian Literature, 1911–1956,* 213).

Literary historian and the doyen of comparative literature in India, Professor Sisir Kumar Das finds the continuing potential for the narrative of *Anandamath* in its thematic appraisal over the years.

> The Indian political novel, appeared in its embryonic form in the historical novel, *Ananda Math* (1882) being the most powerful example. It is not only a construction of the past deliberately distorting the historical facts of the Sannyasi Rebellion which supplies the *Stoff*[1] of the novel, but more a vision for future [*sic*], providing a blue-print, as it were, for the revolutionary organisations to be born in the next century . . . The idea of the secret organization, the identification of the country with divinity, assertion of patriotism as the highest form of religion and the song 'Vandemataram' the paean of the revolutionaries – all were appropriated by different political parties in varying degrees later. In fact this work, though written in the nineteenth century and not acclaimed by critics for aesthetic excellence, became most influential in the twentieth century political history of the country (Das, *A History of Indian Literature, 1911–1956,* 70).

This potential for visualising the unreal firmly places Chatterji's narrative in the disnarrated mould, having held greater socio-political potential for the succeeding century due to authorial predisposition.

Anandamath was certainly designed to arouse patriotism and its ire was directed against the British. But Chatterji never made that intention explicit and much of it remained in the plane of 'what could have been'. The role of disnarration in *Anandamath* is to serve the dual role of denigrating the Muslim rule in trying to envision an alternate universe where it is overthrown by a legion of saints, as well as ushering in British rule and modernity, which

Chatterji hoped his fellow countrymen would accept as beneficial as the Healer tried hard to convince Satyananda. Chatterji would rather make several efforts to camouflage it in subsequent editions. In the first edition published by Radhanath Banerji, Bhabananda would complain of the Raja not protecting the people (Das, *The Artist in Chains,* 157). The defeat of a group of English soldiers also finds mention but in the subsequent versions, the word 'English' would come to be replaced by 'sepoy' (Das, *The Artist in Chains,* 157). In the fourth edition the very word is substituted by the word 'musalman', in an obvious attempt to tone down the criticism of the British administration (Das, *The Artist in Chains,* 157). The Bangadarshan version refers to the sexual exploits of Thomas among the Santhal girls. This would also be deleted in the second edition (Das, *The Artist in Chains,* 157). The Bangadarshan version as well as the first edition of the novel refer to Jibananda's opponents as 'English' but in the next edition, 'English' was replaced by 'yaban' and in some places by 'nede', both terms implying the Muslims, the second term being a pejorative one (Das, *The Artist in Chains,* 157). Even the word 'ingrejder', meaning 'of the English', was changed to 'shatruder' meaning 'of the Enemies' (Das, *The Artist in Chains,* 157). Chatterji would also go on to make a set of historical judgements on the nature and consequences of Muslim rule in Bengal: 'How does our Muslim ruler protect us? We have lost our religion, our caste, our honour and family name, and now are about to lose our lives. . . . How can Hinduism survive unless we drive out these dissolute swine?' (Sarkar 180).

That these seem insidiously authenticated given the power of Chatterji's prose makes us understand the stratagem of the narrative. The annihilation of the Muslims is a repeated call for action in *Anandamath,* just as it is in *Jay Somanatha.*

It is in the light of this that Satyananda's refusal to accept the prophetic vision of the Healer urging the Santans to cede their struggle has to be seen. The disnarrated passage with which the first version of the novel concludes reads:

> The Vishnu temple was now deserted.
> Suddenly the lamps in the temple burned higher.
> And they did not go out.

> The flame that Satyananda had lit before departing did not die out easily.
> If I get the chance, I'll tell you about that some other time. (Chatterji 280)

In this anti-climax can Chatterji's ploy through the disnarrated apparatus be unearthed? that is, of upholding the British rule as a necessary temporary purging of the sins undergone in the regime of Muslim conquerors.

Anandamath was widely translated into almost all the major Indian languages. There exist seven different translations of the book in Hindi alone (Bose 125). Its translations continued unabated for decades after Chatterji's death. Therefore the reception and the renewal of the disnarrated continued while the embedded cultural forms since then have only become far more hegemonic and communal.

Munshi's historicism proves to be a fragmented and fabricated disnarrative bridge, a reframing of truth subject to the inaccurate focalisation of memory. *Jay Somanatha* is the story of a place of pilgrimage – Pattana and the shrine of Shiva located there and how it is decimated by the armies of an invading iconoclast – Mahmud in 1026. It is also the story of the faith of Ganga Sarvajna, the sacrifices and resistance of King Bhimdeva and Samant who defended the temple of Shiva against the invading armies of Mahmud Ghaznavi, and over all, the resilience of a community unified during times of invasion. The allegorical significance of Mahmud's invasion, the defeat of Bhimdeva and the destruction of the temple, to its being rebuilt again, brings about a function of the topoi contrasting plausibility and truth in order to declare itself steeped in reality rather than fiction.

With Munshi's mastery as a storyteller having already become a household name after his trilogy consisting of *Pattani Prabhuta*, *Gujaratno ath* and *Rajadhiraj* was published, *Jay Somanatha* fired the imagination of readers for decades and continues to serve as the meta-narrative of resurgent Hindutva in the face of threat. Perhaps it would be important to remember that Munshi, along with R. C. Majumdar, was the principal editor of Bharatiya Vidya Bhavan's *History and Culture of the Indian People*. As the founder of the Bharatiya Vidya Bhavan (founded 1938), Munshi had sanctioned Majumdar's *History and Culture of the Indian People* (first volume issued 1951) with financial assistance from the Indian Government. The problems with the volume were many, the entire period from c.1200 being considered as one of foreign rule (the Muslims being perceived as foreigners and Hindus as the indigenous people) with the humiliated Hindus looking for an opportunity to slaughter the Mlechhas (the yabans of Chatterji). Majumdar even read the revolt of 1857 as one led by Hindus and saw in the national movement a distorted awakening due to Gandhi's attempts to mollify Muslim sentiments as a result of which the country was portioned. The series itself was conceptualised in a manner so as to give more volumes to what was considered to be periods of glorious Hindu domination, and fewer volumes to what was considered to be periods of Muslim domination. Majumdar himself being a great proponent of Greater India, the indigenous cultures of South-east Asia were ignored while highlighting its Hinduisation.

The communal prejudices inherent in the series were refuted at length by D.D. Kosambi (Habib 85). However, Munshi shared the views of Majumdar and perhaps had a far greater evocative power when it came to his native language Gujarati, and as a politician, could achieve much more. Surprisingly enough, in *Jay Somanatha,* he chose to use the retelling of the event by the Turko-Persian sources to read Mahmud's raid on Somanatha, epitomising the archetypal encounter of Islam with Hindu idolatry. He chooses to overlook the Sanskrit inscriptions wherein no mention is made of Mahmud's attack on the Somanatha temple, which also questions the rhetoric of the Turko-Persian sources (Thapar 86). The explanation given for the decline of the Somanatha temple is its age and mismanagement (Thapar 86). Since there was no major political patron to maintain the temple until Kumarapala decided to look after its upkeep, the temple constructed by Bhimdeva may have deteriorated over time (Thapar 87).

> In reconstructing the history of Somanatha he dates the earliest temple to the start of the Christian era and the second to a rebuilding in the sixth century by the Maitrikas which he says was destroyed by the Arabs. The archaeological evidence differs from these statements. Jaina sources refer to Somanatha as a

> safe area for images prior to the eleventh century. This would not suggest that the temple was subject to repeated raids by Arabs. . . . The archaeological evidence of a temple dates the first structure to the tenth century or possibly at the earliest to the late ninth century. This tenth century temple would have been the one raided by Mahmud.' (Thapar 193–96)

She has further said that the repeated destruction of the temple as mentioned in the Persian sources is also not apparent from the excavation. Munshi himself was a believer in *Sanatan Dharma*, something Chatterji espouses through the cult of the Sanyasis in *Anandamath*. Similarly if Munshi's novels are analysed in continuity, one would notice an attempt to interpret the Indian civilisation, its early history and religious ideals.

The discursive strategies of disnarration reorient the fragmentary or disconnected narrative element towards integration into symbolical embodiment of the authorial ideology. Disnarration, according to Gerald Prince, makes readers more conscious about the different value systems that narrative modes can constitute (Whitmarsh 184). Prince writes: 'The disnarrated guides meaning by constituting a model that allows texts better to define themselves, to specify and emphasize the meanings that they wish to communicate, and to designate the values they develop and aspire to' (*Narrative as Theme,* 38).

Needless to say, much of the negative potential of many passages such as 'Vande Mataram', or the euphoria associated with Somanatha have found continuity through the signified – that of a resurgent Hindu community, fiercely protective of its religious identity in the face of threat, even when the threat is merely a 'what if'. In the case of Chatterji, it would be difficult to say that the authorial intent was communal if one looks at his oeuvre which has also produced characters like Ayesha in the early novels and Chand Shah faqir in his waning years. However, it would also be wrong to say that he was unaware of the various implications of his novel. If it is ahistorical to call his narration as laden with communal propaganda, it would also be irrational to deny the communal stratagem it contained due to discursive practices of the disnarrated within the counterfactual narrative. After his debate with William Hastie, Chatterji would give up on the themes concerning class, caste and gender, and from the 1880s he would start looking for an ethico-religious site within which to locate his Hindu Rashtra, which he begins to identify with collective self-discipline such as that of the Santans and not with freedom (Sarkar 170–74). As Tanika Sarkar has rightly pointed out:

> The themes of class, caste and gender abruptly disappear from his writing, their absence filled by reflections on all that constitutes authentic and fully historicized Hinduism, on the culpability of the Muslim in Indian history, and on how the Hindu nation may be imagined and constructed. For Chattopadhyay now the resolution of social and national malaise seemed to lie in imagining an apocalyptic war with Muslims through which Hindus would ingest their valour and prove their ability to make a nation. (156)

Munshi taps on the same religious fervour and the militaristic potential of the people bound within the geo-political confines of a nation, wherein invented nationalism is laced with religiosity and creates the homogeneous identity of a majority religion.

When Samant and Mehtaji the minister, try to convince Bhimdeva to give the Ghazni a safe passage till Prabhasa Pattana while they await his arrival at Somanatha, Mehtaji cites religious identification and unity being greater than the cohesive bond under a feudal leader.

One of the reasons Damodar Mehta, Bhimdeva's minister, favours fighting Mahmud from Somanatha is because '. . . we would be in our God's shelter there and Gurudev would inspire us. The Rajput warriors would fight for their beloved personal god there and not to save their kingdom. They would not yearn for anything other than a victory in this world or deserved paradise in another' (Munshi, *Jay Somanatha*,154).[2]

The case of Kanhaiyalal Maneklal Munshi was different. An apologetic for a pure Aryan race as the lineage of the Gurjaras and then the Hindus, his artistic consciousness was defined from the very beginning. One must remember that, in 1964, Munshi was the President of the Vishva Hindu Parishad, and took an active role in its foundation and charting its future course. Munshi was also India's Agent-General in Hyderabad when the police action initiated in September 1948, led to a massacre of Muslims. But he does not recount this in his memoirs, *The End of an Era* (1957).[3]

Jay Somanatha contained the roots of Munshi's historical assessment of Mahmud even though it does not paint as negative a picture as Munshi would develop later, imbued with his contempt for the Muslim 'other'. Munshi would become one of the main proponents for the reconstruction of the Somanatha temple, projecting it as a means of liberation from the oppression-ridden past of a community, which he frequently equated with race. Thus, in 1951, Munshi presents his own understanding of the situation '. . . for a thousand years Mahmud's destruction of the shrine has been burnt into the collective sub-conscious of the race, as an unforgettable national disaster . . .' (Munshi, *Somanatha*, 89). To equate the incident from an era when nationalities were non-existent and did not correspond with today's geographical lines, is anachronistic in nature. But Munshi had already spelled out his authorial intent elsewhere in the same book. Yet he knew very well that more than his scholarly attempt, it would be the temporal and spatial domain of the vernacular text which would reward him, by etching his self-proclaimed messianic vision firmly in the minds of his readers and making him quite the household name.

Munshi's narrative apparatus hinges on current fears and absence of stability, amongst large sections of a conglomerate 'Hindu' community, while relying on the denial of the internalised truths of heterodoxy to aid in the realisation and affirmation of their fears. In other words, the disnarrated helps in building up a world of possibility, which is then taken up and sewn together in a socio-political metanarrative by his readers, whose perception of their own present, beginning with Chatterji's reception, had slowly but steadily snowballed into a heady sense of community preservation due to a misguided ever-growing threat perception. The perception of being uprooted from what was rightfully theirs and the fear of again going back to the dark medieval ages of 'Muslim' rule as they had come to believe, is what Chatterji's narrative builds around and Munshi's narrative carefully constructs. The latter, however, expects much more conformity and therefore there is a sense of surety in his work as opposed to the absences in Chatterji.

With regard to the reconstruction of Somanatha, Munshi often spoke of the new structure as being associated with the Government of India, and thought of it as an ideal action to embalm the collective subconscious of the nation more than any other activities of the Government. The assent of the then Home Minister and a Congressman from Gujarat, Sardar Vallabhai Patel, according to Munshi, converted Somanatha into an icon of the resurgence of Hindu nationalism, and of freedom from centuries of tyrannical 'Muslim' foreign rule. Recently, claims have been made that Nehru regarded the rebuilding of the temple at Somanatha as a matter of national sentiment, and that the temple was financed by the government. While Vallabhai Patel certainly supported the reconstruction of the temple, Nehru wholeheartedly opposed the idea of the reconstruction and went out of his way to ensure that the Government of India did not become party to religious sentiments. Unfortunately, however, many of his pleas would fall on deaf ears.

The President of India, Rajendra Prasad, had written to Nehru saying that he had been invited to preside over the opening of the new temple and wished to do so, and went ahead with his plans even though Nehru clearly wished otherwise (Guha 131–32). In his reply to Rajendra Prasad, Nehru wrote: 'I confess that I do not like the idea of your associating yourself with a spectacular opening of the Somanatha temple. This is not merely visiting a temple, but rather participating in a significant function which unfortunately has a number of implications . . . I feel that it would be better if you did not preside over this function' (Nehru, *Letters*). Even in Europe, between 1730 and 1830, historians would often be trained as jurists and theologians, while some would take up writing as an avocation being primarily dedicated to their service as bankers and bureaucrats (Smith 1150–76). This meant that with little institutional power on the side of historians and a formal method yet to develop, one would see the research of the Benedictine monks and scholars of the University of Gottingen alongside the historical novels of Walter Scott (Smith 1150–76). Before a professional historian's scope, corpus, mode and method were defined, everything from epic poetry, historical play to journalism and the romance fiction could have sufficed as historical narratives. Chatterji's thought was not much out of place given that many in his literary milieu experienced a similar battle, having taken up their pens guided by the need of historical enterprise. Many litterateurs were trying to take up the role of professional historians, and often the output was, as one can expect, literary texts which for many were the embodiment of their historical consciousness. Gobind Chandra Sen, Peary Chand Mitra, M. C. Deb and many more, had similar opinions which guided their world view.

If Chatterji's literary corpus, under the guise of the romance fiction of Scott, takes his own emblematic study of culture through invented traditions where evidence mattered little, Munshi would continue with the romantic tradition of finding historical traces in monuments, ancient ruins, pilgrimage places and folk tales which had taken strong roots by then. Not only was Chatterji well aware of the traditional sources citing the role of the Fakirs; even Munshi as an avowed Hindutva theologian would certainly have been aware of what the Sanskrit sources cited. It is therefore, their distinct politico-cultural ideology which is envisioned throughout the narrative, and to aid in which the disnarrated becomes the writer's tool.

Sisir Kumar Das has delineated this admixture as born out of the Indian tryst with the European conception of history and canons. It is during the course of this encounter wherein the hitherto non-existent distinction between historical consciousness and legends was felt.

> A distinction between the 'historical imagination', and the 'mythical imagination' the former supported by facts and evidences, and the latter sustained by a perception of past or by racial memory was a nineteenth-century phenomenon. What distinguished the literary historical writings was the conscious attempt to reconstruct the past according to contemporary needs under the compulsions of a colonial rule . . . The early historical works in various Indian languages, such as biographies or accounts of holy places or of regions, contained considerable amount of anecdotes and 'fanciful' materials which were incorporated by the writers without any qualms. When historical writings began in India by Indian scholars

> themselves, they followed the existing trends of historiography in England . . . The early writers created characters many of whom were anachronistic, and described situations and events which were completely imaginary. Their readers never questioned their authenticity but remained enamoured by the magic of the reconstruction. (Das, *History of Indian Literature, 1911–1956*, 94–95)

Therefore we see that the externally focussed counterfactuals that I have discussed here are a hypothetical alteration in a past sequence of events that changes the events in a factual sequence in order to create a different, counterfactual outcome (Dannenberg 119). Both of the novels are conceptualised in the manner of what could have been. In the words of Prince:

> In underscoring the displayable nature of narrative, its qualities of an object calling for contemplation, exploration and response, the disnarrated shows that narrative is not only a matter of counting, accounting and recounting, but also one of discounting. It insists upon the ability to conceive and manipulate hypothetical worlds or states of affairs and the freedom to reject various models of intelligibility, of coherence and significance, various norms, conventions or codes for world and fiction-making. It institutes an anti-model in terms of which the text defines itself and indicates the aesthetics it develops and espouses, the audience it represents and aspires to, the matters, topics and configurations, the audience takes to be tellable. (Prince, 'The Disnarrated', 6)

The theme of historical revenge and the seething discontent and deep-seeded animosity between two groups antagonistic to each other (in this context one is often posited as indigenous and the 'other' constructed as the invader) has forever been placed against the known history of heterogeneity and plurality, the Indianisation that followed Islam in its shift from the Perso-Islamic context or the way the term 'Hindu' beginning as a geographical marker has remained amorphous in most quarters until the advent of the colonisers. Surprisingly enough, as Romila Thapar has pointed out, one finds no mention of Ghazni's raids in Kalhana's *Rajatarangini* wherein Ghazni's military campaigns against the Shahis finds mention (Thapar 106). The non-Persian sources as she further points out 'do not refer to the raid, nor provide evidence of a trauma among the Hindus which was said to have resulted from the raid . . .' (Thapar x). Having slighted Sanskritic sources, the very high culture of which he is supposed to be a torchbearer and whose resurgence he saw in the rebuilding of the Somanatha temple, one may ask whether Munshi remains true to his ideological predisposition, if not his craft. This is not a case of event gaining primacy over meaning, or meaning over event but events which were constructed through the disnarrated mode of unrealised possibility containing all the ingredients of 'epistemic expressions of ignorance . . . purely imagined worlds, desired worlds, or intended worlds, unfulfilled expectations, unwarranted beliefs, failed attempts, crushed hopes, suppositions and false calculations, errors and lies' (Prince, *Narrative as Theme,* 32). Therefore even while Mahmud's role as an iconoclast is highlighted and harped on time and again, the rivalry between Jainism and Shaivism remains in the sphere of the non-narrated. Trade profits for Veraval through the trade with the Arabian Peninsula or the Persian Gulf, or for that matter the looting of the pilgrims by the Abhiras, Yadavas and Chudasamas are also summarily ignored. The latter is cursorily hinted at when Munshi writes about Bhimdeva following the iron rule of Moolrajdeva of the Chalukya clan, which had brought uniformity and allegiance to the throne in and around Pattana (Munshi, *Jay Somanatha,*142). But that is all.

The response of the common reader is always guided by the skill of the narration than by the fidelity of the author to facts. This is where the narration of Chatterji and Munshi have both successfully held the attention of their readers, all the while luring them into a world of possibility, a world which is mostly populated and made up of 'what could have been'. It is in this context that alternative propositions even when posited as real need to be reconsidered within the disnarrated mould. In an age of ruptured histories and displaced identities, both the authors studied here try to satiate the reader's longing for forgotten history by juxtaposing an individual's memory of the past with what they came to believe as the popular notion of history. Functioning in a world far away from the scrutiny of academia or the responsibilities of having to stand testimony to historical veracity, there is more than one commonality between Chatterji and Munshi's mode of writing and approach towards fiction. This is what unites them even when the most prolific years of their lives are separated by decades.

Notes

1. the subject or thematic matter, drawing on their semblance with human existence
2. This and other translations from the Hindi version are mine. A translation of the same in English by former ICS officer, H. M. Patel, was published by Bharatiya Vidya Bhavan but has been out of print for a long time now. It wasn't available to me while writing this paper.
3. Noorani, A.G., 'Of a Massacre Untold', *Frontline,* 3 March 2001, accessed 11 December 2014, http://www.frontline.in/static/html/fl1805/18051130.htm. This has been further elaborated in A. G. Noorani in *The Destruction of Hyderabad.* (New Delhi: Tulika Books, 2013).

WORKS CITED

Bandyopadhyay, Sekhar. *From Plassey to Partition: A History of Modern India.* New Delhi: Orient Longman, 2004. Print.

Bose, S.K. *Bankimcandra Chatterji.* New Delhi: Government of India, Publications Division, 1974. Print.

Chatterji, Bankimcandra. *Anandamath or The Sacred Brotherhood.* Trans. Julius J. Lipner. New York: Oxford UP, 2005. Print.

Das, Sisir Kumar. *A History of Indian Literature: Western Impact: Indian Response, 1800–1910.* New Delhi: Sahitya Akademi, 1991. Print.

———. *A History of Indian Literature 1911–1956.* New Delhi: Sahitya Akademi, 1995. Print.

———. *The Artist in Chains: The Life of Bankimchandra Chatterji.* New Delhi: New Statesman Publishing, 1984. Print.

Dannenberg, Hilary P. *Coincidence and Counterfactuality: Plotting Time and Space in Narrative Fiction.* Lincoln: U of Nebraska P, 2008. Print.

Dasgupta, Atis Kumar. *The Fakir and Sannyasi Uprisings*. Calcutta: K. P. Bagchi & Co., 1992. Print.

Guha, Ramachandra. *India After Gandhi: History of the World's Largest Democracy*. London: Pan Books, 2008. Print.

Habib, Irfan, 'Kosambi, Marxism and Indian History.' *Economic and Political Weekly* 43 (2008): 85–88. Print.

Hunter, William Wilson. *The Annals of Rural Bengal*. New York: Leypoldt and Holt, 1868.

Joshi, Priya. *In Another Country: Colonialism, Culture and the English Novel in India*. New York: Columbia UP, 2002. Print.

Karttunen, Laura. 'A Sociostylistic Perspective on Negatives and the Disnarrated: Lahiri, Roy, Rushdie.' *Partial Answers: Journal of Literature and the History of Ideas* 6.2 (2008): 419–41. Print.

Kaviraj, Sudipta. *The Unhappy Consciousness: Bankimchandra Chattopadhyay and the Formation of Nationalist Discourse in India*. Delhi: Oxford UP, 1995. Print.

Meister, Jan Christoph. *Computing Action: A Narratological Approach*. Berlin; New York: Walter De Gruyter, 2003. Print.

Munshi, K. M. *Jay Somanatha*. Trans. Padmasingh Sharma Kamlesh. New Delhi: Rajkamal Prakashan, 1993. Print.

———. *Somanatha: The Shrine Eternal*. Bombay: Bharatiya Vidya Bhavan, 1965. Print.

Nehru, Jawaharlal. Letters to Rajendra Prasad, 2 March 1951, C. Rajagopalachari Papers, Fourth Instalment, NMML. Quoted in Ramachandra Guha. *India After Gandhi*. London: Pan Books, 2008. Print.

Noorani, A.G. 'Of a Massacre Untold,' *Frontline*, 18.5 (3–6 March 2001). Web. <http://www.frontline.in/static/html/fl1805/18051130.htm>

Prince, Gerald. *Narrative as Theme: Studies in French Fiction*. Lincoln: U of Nebraska P, 1992. Print.

———. 'The Disnarrated.' *Style*. 22.1 (Spring 1988): 1–8.

———. 'Revisiting Narrativity.' In *Telling Performances: Essays on Gender, Narrative & Performance*. Eds. Brian Nelson, Anne Freadman and Philip Anderson. New Jersey: Associated University Presses, 2001. Print.

Ryan, Marie-Laure. *Narrative As Virtual Reality*. Baltimore: Johns Hopkins University, 2001. Print.

Sarkar, Tanika. *Hindu Wife, Hindu Nation: Community, Religion and Cultural Nationalism*. Delhi: Permanent Black, 2001. Print.

Sharma, R.S. 'Communalism and India's Past.' *Social Scientist* 18 (1990): 3–12. Print.

Smith, Bonnie G. 'Gender and the Practices of Scientific History: The Seminar and Archival Research in the Nineteenth Century.' *American Historical Review* 100 (1995): 1150–76. Print.

Thapar, Romila. *Somanatha: The Many Voices of a History*. New Delhi: Penguin Books India, 2004. Print.

Whitmarsh, Tim. *Narrative and Identity in the Ancient Greek Novel: Returning Romance*. Cambridge: Cambridge UP, 2011. Print.

His Story, Her Story and History

Competing Stories in Louise Erdrich's *Tracks*

David Jeyaraj Franklin

The story . . . comes up different every time, and has no ending, no beginning. They get the middle wrong too. They only know they don't know anything. (Erdrich 31)

When a community faces the ultimate crisis – the crisis of culture – it is posed with just two options; to swim upstream, on most occasions in vain, or to allow to be washed by the currents of cultural change. Native American writer of Anishinaabe heritage, Louise Erdrich captures her community at such a crossroads in her 1988 novel, *Tracks*. All the nine chapters of the novel tell the story of the Chippewas set against the historical background of the tumultuous seasons of 1912 to 1924. (The Chippewas, also known as the Ojibwas or the Anishinaabe people, are one of the largest Native American communities of North America.)

The real story begins with the implementation of the Dawes Act in 1887, which wanted the natives of the country to assimilate into the mainstream white European culture in exchange for their acceptance of land parcels and giving up on hunting. The tax regime comes into effect twenty-five years later, resulting in land loss, culture loss, and as a result, placing the Indian community at the crossroads of culture. '*Tracks* is about the catastrophic losses that have left the characters . . . wandering in Erdrich's vaguely defined terrain' (Owens 215). Shelley Reid believes that it is the story of 'the Native American identity, the connection of an individual with the history of his or her tribe' (16).

The Competing Narrators of *Tracks*

The two narrators of the novel are the elderly Nanapush who reminds himself and others of the trickster Nanabozho, and the teenaged girl of mixed descent, Pauline Puyat. Both the narrators 'stand at opposite extremes to each other and speak with noticeably distinct voices' (Piccolo 120) to tell their versions of the story with very personal agendas – Nanapush trying to reconcile the teenaged listener Lulu to her mother Fleur and Pauline trying to justify her cultural transformation and her hatred towards the indigenous lives of Fleur and others.

The entire story is set in the early decades of the 20th century in a fictional Indian reservation in the state of North Dakota. Historically speaking, this was the period of change in the Native American way of life as many families who got allotments decades earlier, were slowly losing their land either to the government on tax defaults or to the lumbering agencies in exchange for petty consumables. This was also the period of mass deaths due to consumption. At the end of this period, Nanapush finds himself an elder at a relatively young age of fifty. He tells the story of Fleur to her daughter Lulu trying to persuade her back to Indian ways of life. He details his struggles to save Fleur from consumption, the land from the government and the loggers, and the younger generation from getting Americanised.

On the other hand, Pauline Puyat, the second narrator, comes into the picture with multiple agendas. A teenaged girl of mixed descent, she desires to convert Fleur and other natives into the mainstream culture. She goes further deep into the coloniser's religion of Christianity and later tries to achieve sainthood by forcing herself into a self-punishing mode of Catholicism. Though she appears to be the Western voice in the novel, she is also jealous of Fleur and her native powers and also desires to lure Fleur's husband Eli Kashpaw. Pauline had earlier abandoned the Chippewa way of life, strongly believing and advocating that 'to hang back was to perish' (Erdrich 14).

Gerald Prince's argument that 'something is not told (at least for a while) not so much because of a narratorial incapacity, a tellability imperative, a "legal" imposition, but because of some narrative call for rhythm, characterization, suspense, surprise, and so on' (Prince 2) holds good for this narrative as each of the two authors presses for their stories with personal manifestos. Caught between these two diametrically opposite narrators, the storyline of *Tracks* struggles between the two extremes of reality.

The two narrators compete with each other to push forth their version of the story. For instance, when Nanapush tells Fleur that

'Pauline Puyat's home again. . . . She tells a story' indicating the Argus incident, Fleur cries out, 'Uncle, the Puyat lies' (Erdrich 38). Laura Tanner's observation that 'the act of violation' remains present 'only in Pauline's imagination' (Tanner 117) endorses Prince's argument that 'one narrator's unnarratable can very well be another's narratable just as what is impossible in one context may be *de rigueur* in another one' (Prince 2).

The absolute disregard for Pauline's versions of the story by Nanapush and other like-minded characters in the novel is brought out by the ruminations of Nanapush about his co-narrator:

> She was, to my mind, an unknown mixture of ingredients, like pale bannock that sagged or hardened. We never knew what to call her, or where she fit or how to think when she was around. So we tried to ignore her, and that worked as long as she was quiet. But she was different once her mouth opened and she started to wag her tongue. She was worse than Nanapush, in fact. For while I was careful with my known facts, she was given to improving the truth. (Erdrich 39)

The reader of this text is often made to believe in Nanapush's versions and not Pauline's because of the implied motives behind their narrations. While Nanapush has set for himself the 'high priestly' task of being the culture-police of his community and tries to bring Lulu back into the fold, Pauline's monologues are presented as self-justifications for all that she did in the near past. Also contributing to this distrust that Pauline earns for herself is her own absence of conviction in her narrations. She often 'relive(s) . . . over and over' (Erdrich 66) certain key moments. But on another instance she appears confused as to whether her narrations were true at all: 'Sometimes, thinking back, I see my arms lift, my hands grasp, see myself dropping the beam into the metal grip. At other times, the moment is erased' (Erdrich 28). She also blames Margaret Kashpaw, Eli's mother, for her telling the stories in particular ways.

> It was because of Margaret Kashpaw's scheming. She pulled the truth or some version of it out of me, I don't know how, then despised me because I was too weak to resist her. When I left the Kashpaw house, I felt both heavier and lighter. I was lighter

> because I had unburdened my shoulders, and heavier because I knew the dreams would fall. (Erdrich 65)

Another reason for Pauline's apparent unreliability with her narration is her inability to connect with the older world while Nanapush is able to connect to both the worlds – the mystic pre-colonial native life in the woods as well as the contemporary realities of colonial government and bureaucracy. Either realising that it is impossible to cohabit with the powers of the woods or out of fear for them, Pauline runs away from the windigos, the water man Misshepeshu, and other supernatural characters to hide herself in the robes offered to her at the catholic nunnery. There she tries to strike a balance between her past and her present by claiming visions. She uses her version of the Virgin Mary's interference in the life of poor Sophie to 'make her claim to the power' (Stookey 78) of miracle healing, which she claims to counter the apparent popularity of Fleur's mysticism.

The triangular relationship between the three main characters of the novel – Nanapush, Pauline, and Fleur – also contributes to the way the story has been narrated. While Nanapush shares a platonic love for Fleur, even going to the level of giving his name to Fleur's daughter of unknown parentage, Pauline trudges nervously on the boundaries of companionship, rivalry, and at times absolute scorn at the central character, whose story she tries to narrate.

The Native American tradition of telling stories about the history they just witnessed is obvious when Nanapush talks about the burden of carrying the stories. To him, they are passed on to the listeners as Pauline did to Margaret. He also believes that Pauline keeps telling these stories to herself as he identifies her as 'playing the parts of both addresser and addressee' (Erdrich 52). Catherine Rainwater in her assessment of the novel regards this technique as a 'self-conscious accommodation of cultural outsiders in the audience, and thus converts "reader" to "listener" ' (145) while Reid argues that 'the relationship between the two narrators is more antagonistic; although they tell stories that overlap and complement each other, Pauline and Nanapush speak from vantage points that differ in gender, generation, and community standing', often scoffing at each other (10).

The Disnarrated in *Tracks*

Gerald Prince defines 'disnarrated' as consisting of 'hopes, desires, imaginings, ponderings, unreasonable expectations and incorrect beliefs' (4). He also believes that it 'can also help to define a narrator, his or her narratee and their relationship' as well as 'contribute to the development of a theme'(5).

The novel *Tracks* opens with the scene of Nanapush saving Fleur Pillager from the TB- infested cabin in the woods. With a chivalric effort, he saves her but fears the revenge of the dead for taking away the young girl from their company.

> We feared that they would hear us and never rest, come back out of pity for the loneliness we felt. They would sit in the snow outside the door, waiting until from longing we joined them. We would all be together on the journey then, our destination the village at the end of the road where people gamble day and night but never lose their money, eat but never fill their stomach, drink but never leave their minds. (Erdrich 5)

Nanapush follows up this description of the native purgatory with an even more impressive narration of his deliberations with the dead which was in vain: '. . . they must abandon us. I insisted. But the Pillagers were as stubborn as the Nanapush clan and would not leave my thoughts. I thought they followed me home. All the way down the trail, just beyond the edges of my sight, they flickered, thin as needles, shadows piercing shadows' (Erdrich 6).

These incidents written down in great dramatic detail fit Gerald Prince's definition of his coinage, 'disnarrated': they are terms, phrases, and passages that consider what did not or does not take place. Nanapush visualises and even narrates the incident that he imagined to have happened, but in reality (as he himself accepts), did not happen.

Pauline in her account of an attempted rape of Fleur by her workmates in the Argus meat-shop tells what she should have done to stop the brutality. 'This is when I should have gone to Fleur, saved her, thrown myself on Dutch the way Russell did once he unlocked my arms' (Erdrich 26). This is followed by a brutal tornado that devastates property in the town with no casualties until the bodies of the rapists were found in a locker closed from outside. Pauline describes their faces as 'set in concentration, mouths open as if to speak some careful thought, some agreement they'd come to in each other's arms' (30). Pauline describes Fleur's life post the rape at Argus in plain terms as if compiling the many versions of the rumour-mill: 'Some say she married the water man, Misshepeshu, or that she lives in shame with white men or windigos, or that she's killed them all' (31).

Nanapush tries to find lies in Pauline's stories. To him, as Pauline lies and tries to 'describe things she had not seen, her fingers wandered in the air, her voice screeched'. He even passes a judgement over her abilities to tell the truth when he observes that 'she was born a liar, and sure to die one. The practice of deception was so constant with her that it got to be a kind of truth' (Erdrich 25).

The author deliberately uses seasons and years as the titles of the chapters. Through this method, she tries to push in a semblance of linearity in narration, whereas by focus, point of view, and by the choice of incidents, the two narrators make it appear two completely different stories. In Piccolo's words, 'we are finally left with . . . a realization of the inevitable ambiguity inherent in any accurate presentation of events' (121). As Susan Perez Castillo observes, 'the reader shuttles between, not two different perceptions of reality, but two diametrically different realities' (294). As Mandella argues, this dual narrative, presented by the duelling narrators, offers the readers a splendid tale. Like the two diametrically opposite points providing a central point where one can expect the reality, Erdrich's tale presents the two sides of the coin of truth, projecting a reality that lies somewhere in between.

In terms of the narrative techniques of the novel, Erdrich is successful in 'creating a situation' which, in Prince's words, 'emphasizes the realities of representation as opposed to the representation of realities' (5). In Nanapush's own words, 'Only looking back is there a pattern. . . . There is a story to it the way there is a story to all, never visible while it is happening. Only after, when an old man sits dreaming and talking in his chair, the design springs clear' (Erdrich 34). This pattern, like the fabled secret of Robert Frost, makes the readers dance round in a ring, and suppose while it sits in the middle and knows.

WORKS CITED

Castillo, Susan Perez. 'Postmodernism, Native American Literature and the Real: The Silko-Erdrich Controversy.' *The Massachusetts Review* 31.2 (Summer 1991): 285–94. Print.

Erdrich, Louise. *Tracks: A Novel.* New York: Henry Holt, 1988. Print.

Frost, Robert. 'The Secret Sits.' *Poemhunter*: n.p. Web. 22 Jan. 2013.

Mandella. 'The Effect of Dueling Narrators in Louise Erdrich's *Tracks*.' *Everything2*. Everything2 Media LLC, n.d. Web. 25 Jan. 2013.

Owens, Louis. *Other Destinies: Understanding the American Indian Novel.* Norman: U of Oklahoma, 1992. Print.

Piccolo, Anthony. 'It Comes Up Different Every Time: Narrative Point of View in Louise Erdrich's *Tracks*.' *Philologia* 42 (2011): 119–35. Print.

Prince, Gerald. 'The Disnarrated.' *Style* 22.1 (Spring 1988): 1–8. Print.

Rainwater, Catherine. 'Ethnic Signs in Erdrich's *Tracks* and *The Bingo Palace*.' In *The Chippewa Landscape of Louise Erdrich*. Ed. Allan Richard Chavkin. Tuscaloosa: U of Alabama, 1999. 144–60. Print.

Reid, Shelley E. 'The Stories We Tell: Louise Erdrich's Identity Naratives.' In *Native American Writers*. Ed. Harold Bloom. Philadelphia: Chelsea House, 1998. 5–23. Print.

Smith, Jeanne Rosier. *Writing Tricksters: Mythic Gambols in American Ethnic Literature*. Berkeley: U of California, 1997. Print.

Stookey, Lorena Laura. *Louise Erdrich: A Critical Companion*. Westport, CT: Greenwood, 1999. Print.

Tanner, Laura E. *Intimate Violence: Reading Rape and Torture in Twentieth-Century Fiction*. Bloomington: Indiana UP, 1994. Print.

Tricksters, Rebels and Wandering Narratives in Thomas King's *Green Grass, Running Water*

Anushka Sen

Green Grass, Running Water begins with the performance of storytelling, which, in itself is not particularly striking. Perhaps more curious is the fact that the first narrator to be identified by name–the Lone Ranger–makes no less than four inaccurate starts before his story can take off. Three out of four of these failed attempts are built upon a stock opening, such as 'Once upon a time' (9)[1], which the Lone Ranger abandons after its suitability is questioned by his audience. These occurrences bear a resemblance to the 'disnarrated' (Prince), a narrative technique categorised by Gerald Prince, in which a possibility suggested by or in the narrative, for itself, is left uncharted. Although Prince cites multiple uses of the disnarrated, this instance in King's novel does not seamlessly fit any of Prince's definitions. Prince sums up the concept of the disnarrated thus — 'the category that. . . covers all the events that do not happen but, nonetheless, are referred to (in a negative or hypothetical mode) by the narrative text' (Prince 299). This includes references to possibilities that are presented as 'unrealized' (299) at their inception itself, such as the sentence – 'she ran faster than any of her companions could have' (quoted in Prince 299). The disnarrated may also involve an extended process, in which a character's imaginings are eventually contradicted by the fictitious reality of the narrative. In the case of the Lone Ranger, the alternate openings are not framed by speculation or denial within the utterance. It is after he has spoken with apparent conviction that they are negated by an external agent, the listeners, thus also taking the burden of refusal or abstinence off the extended narrative. These are conditions not considered by Gerald Prince in his essay. Nonetheless, in this paper, I will place the aforementioned impediments to storytelling on the terrain of the disnarrated since they do fundamentally deal with unexplored possibilities. The aim of this paper however, is not to read King's text within the framework of disnarration, but to explore how King's use of the disnarrative deviates from Prince's theoretical framework. The focus will not be on the minute structural differences, but upon King's political and aesthetic vision as played out in the entire narrative of *Green Grass, Running Water*, and the special role of the disnarrated in the literary world he creates.

The Lone Ranger's discarded openings, with their conventional phrasing and brevity, hardly offer substantial visions of a deviant narrative. King's variation on the disnarrated here does not therefore tantalise the reader with possibilities as much as create a sense of multiple storytelling traditions. This may be seen as King's attempt to highlight 'the narrating rather than the narrated' and draw attention to an inventive 'narrational strategy' (301), which is one of the specified functions of the disnarrated. In the title of this paper, the phrase 'Wandering Narratives' is on the same plane as 'Tricksters' and 'Rebels', thus implying a fair amount of agency on the part of what is more often an object under discussion. Indeed, the narrative in *Green Grass, Running Water* has quite a potency of its own, which is destabilising from a purely structural point of view, while also allowing chaotic elements in the thematic content of the novel. To make sense of this claim, it is perhaps necessary to take a detour by dwelling upon the novel's narrative structure and its peculiarities.

The book has four main sections, which are presented as the accounts delivered by four Native American or 'Indian'[2] figures respectively – The Lone Ranger, Ishmael, Robinson Crusoe and Hawkeye, in that order. Initially, the Indians appear to be outside a spatio-temporal frame, and their accounts are unravelled in an unspecified realm. Soon enough however, their presence haunts the contemporary and contextualised narrative strand of the book. This primarily 'real-time' narrative involves an extended Indian family, and traces the movement of their individual members, finally coming to a head at the traditional Sun Dance ceremony where the relatives reunite. Simultaneously, we learn of an investigation into the sudden disappearance of four Indians from a hospital for the mentally unstable. Eventually, we see that these fugitive Indians tie up with the characters of the Lone Ranger, Ishmael, Crusoe and Hawkeye, thus combining the eternal and dimensionless with the localised.

Also beyond the boundaries of time and space are an unnamed first-person narrator (who will henceforth be referred to as the I-narrator) and Coyote. Even before the book is divided into its segments, the I-narrator introduces Coyote and the two embark on a conversation that filters through the contemporary narrative every now and then. Their exchange is built around the I-narrator's attempt to tell various creation stories. The liberties taken with punctuation and the use of present tense in their exchange may point away from the typical framework of a dialogue, but Coyote's relentless interjections make the whole process of storytelling transparent. We also get the impression that telling the stories actually causes the events to unfold, or at least allows the storytellers to act as witnesses. For example, at one point in the Lone Ranger's story where there is a reference to the presence of food, Coyote remarks,'that food certainly smells good' (42), hinting at the tangibility of the story-world. Such a technique also enables Coyote to appear in the later stages of the contemporary narrative, and work hand in hand with the Indians to influence the action there.

As for the creation myths, we are given four major variations, each of which is dominated by a female figure – First Woman, Changing Woman, Thought Woman and Sky Woman respectively – though there is the possibility that it is the same woman who goes through these evolutionary stages. Each of them falls through the sky, we are told, and their subsequent escapades involve parodying some aspect of the Genesis story. We learn how each of these women is arrested and imprisoned on some pretext, and eventually makes her escape by donning a disguise – that of the Lone Ranger, Ishamel, Crusoe and Hawkeye respectively.

As if this wasn't enough, the act of storytelling itself is shown to be fraught with difficulties. The four Indian storytellers show up one aspect of the problem to ludicrous extremes – that of beginning. Take the case of Lone Ranger. Before he can delve into the story he has to get past random interruptions – such as 'Hawkeye doesn't have a nice shirt' (8), debate about whose turn it is, and a consensus on the appropriate opening line. We learn that though '[E]verybody makes mistakes', it is '[B]est not to make them with stories' (10). Nonetheless, one never feels a sense of great foreboding and we recall that the same warning has been applied by the character of Norma to interior decoration, that is, it is best not to make mistakes 'with carpet' (8). This lightheartedness prevails through all the confusion, and the arbitrarily yet ritually discarded possibilities bear no tragic overtones, thus diffusing the problem of significant choices and their often destructive repercussions.

Coyote himself is a most frustrating listener. He draws attention to irrelevant details, asks too many questions and is overhasty in warding off possible accusations. In trying to cater to all his demands, the I-narrator is forced to revise his stories, which may suggest that there is a narrative logic, and consequently, right and wrong choices. However, by the end of the book's first segment, he is brought back to his very first statement – 'In the beginning there was nothing. Just the water' (107), a statement echoed by characters within the contemporary narrative as well. This circularity does not of course stop the stories from proceeding but it does prevent the narrative from settling into a purely progression-oriented rhythm.

To say after all this that the narrative is flexible would be a severe understatement. The ease with which it allows deviations, jumps, reconciliations and the interweaving of voices is positively exhilarating; and through these unexpected shifts, the narrative acquires life in a more than rhetorical sense, seeming to generate, rather than contain, the playful and subversive tendencies within the novel. Certainly the narrative technique draws attention to itself and disnarration is one of the techniques used in the process, but disnarration in the conventional sense does not feature prominently in the narrative. However, Coyote's interruptions often refer to canonical narratives that *Green Grass, Running Water* has parodied–a reminder that the novel has taken alternative paths. For example, when Changing Woman identifies a whale as Moby-Jane, Coyote along with the character of Ahab, asserts that 'she means Moby-Dick. . . I read the book' (220). Apart from these interruptions, there are numerous occasions in which a character is about to speak but gets distracted before the story can even begin, stretching the idea of narrative potential to its limit. We have already suggested that the narrative draws attention to its own strategy, which is one of the purposes served by disnarration. Furthermore, Prince writes that:

> In underscoring the 'displayable' nature of narrative. . . its qualities of an object calling for contemplation, exploration, and response, the disnarrated shows that narrative is not only a matter of counting, accounting, and recounting, but also one of discounting. It insists upon the ability to conceive and manipulate hypothetical worlds or states of affairs and the freedom to reject various forms of intelligibility, of coherence and significance, various forms, conventions or codes for world- and fiction-making. (Prince 302)

This description seems to hold true for King's narrative. However, when Prince talks more specifically about the 'explicitly metafictional text', he says that it 'resorts to the disnarrated mainly on the level of discourse in order to insist on its own artificiality. . . in order to foreground the production of a world by language' (303). The slippery nature of a world created and understood through language is indeed made explicit by King, who writes that '[T]here are no truths . . . Only stories' (432), but the word 'artificiality' is somehow not entirely appropriate. The word has a touch of cynicism about it, even if unintended by Prince, which is slightly at odds with the productive energy and restorative good humour that prevail in *Green Grass, Running Water*. The humour does play a part in exposing the artificiality of certain discourses but the narrative in general thrives upon its own abundance and fluidity.

The lack of rigidity in the narrative of *Green Grass, Running Water* is in keeping with the ambivalence in various aspects of the subject matter itself, such as the androgynous character of the Indians, or Alberta, who cannot and does not want to choose between her two lovers. It appears that King is drawn to the status of the in-between, and his novel *Medicine River* too features a woman who, like Alberta, wants a baby without a husband and defies expectations of marriage throughout the novel. What helps drive home the point about fluidity and balance is the profusion of water in the novel. As Coyote pontificates, in his disarming style: 'Hmmmm . . . All this water imagery must mean something' (391), and Thomas King is not bashful about providing the obvious answers.

Water is also integrally associated with the character of Eli Stands Alone and his long, hard resistance to the building of a dam. Though he successfully stalls the project, the dam's destruction is eventually inextricable from his own. It is through this character that the qualities of strength and intransigence are celebrated for a change, and that King explicitly reveals his political alignment against white capitalist privilege. Yet, Eli is not exactly a tragic figure. The earthquake-flood that causes his death as well as the dam's collapse takes place under comical circumstances – that is, Coyote's dancing gets out of hand. At the beginning of *Green Grass, Running Water*, we learn that Eli had adopted the lifestyle of a white man for years, and found it difficult to come home. This – his real crisis as it were – is resolved by his return to the community in no less a capacity than that of rebel *for* their cause. Eli is ultimately consumed by the freshly released water, a levelling force in which there is no hostility, nor the remoteness of divine justice. There is also some consolation in the fact that the cabin which he has occupied for so long will be rebuilt by his family members. Eventually, the harmonising role played by nature, myth and community eclipses the focused energy of hero, mission and resistance.

Moreover, there are a number of reconciliations in the narrative. Alberta does not have to make a clear choice, and her desire for a child minus the baggage of husband is fulfilled through Coyote's magic. Lionel finally outgrows his desire to be a cowboy and steps up in defense of tradition at the Sundance. The escaped Indians eventually return to the Hospital, where the doctor and janitor seem familiar with this ritual of escape and adventure. King's politics therefore is not antagonistic, despite the fact that he uses breaks as part of his artistic technique, and calls attention to unjust ruptures and erasures in history.

In the first of five lectures he delivers under the heading, 'The Truth about Stories' (*Massey Lectures*), he posits the indigenous American world view against the Christian, saying that the former shows a movement from chaos to harmony, whereas the latter is invested in the idea of a fall. In *Green Grass, Running Water*, King uses his cheerful but incisive humour to deflate persistent tropes within white supremacist discourse – such as the heroic cowboy and fetishised Indian, the imperialist entrepreneurship of Crusoe, and most importantly, the myth of Genesis. Theology offers King the opportunity for countless caricatures, ranging from Ahdamn as a choice of name for the first man, to the depiction of GOD as a dream that got loose and now suffers from delusions of grandeur. Yet, King's creation of a highly sentient and polyphonic world, which lies outside conventional boundaries of space and time and is guided by principles of communal harmony, constitutes as much of a challenge to hegemony as his more obvious satire. Perhaps it is even more important as it actually offers the vision of a desirable condition. It must be noted that community here extends beyond its human members. At frequent junctures in the novel, characters are asked to 'mind . . . [their] relations', which alerts them to the need for graceful and considerate behavior. This innocuous phrase, along with the running joke about all Indians being related, points towards a full-fledged indigenous world view, at the heart of which lies the interdependence of all life forms.

Indeed, it is this world view which does not sit easily within the confines of Prince's essay. This becomes more evident when we attempt to read *Green Grass, Running Water* in the context of Prince's views on disnarration in the twentieth century. Prince writes that one of the outcomes of the twentieth century's 'assault on narrative and on history as narrative' is 'a lack of hierarchical distinction between several narrative lines of development'. That is to say, 'all of the narrated is hypothetical, all of it becomes disnarrated' (303). Though Prince is talking primarily about French twentieth century writers here, the question may be legitimately posed – is everything in the narrative of *Green Grass, Running Water* disnarrated? The 'lack of hierarchical distinction' between different narrative strands is fairly explicit in the novel, where despite claims that the story must be told again so we can 'get it right' (107), no version of the story subsumes or contradicts another. However, the different worlds in *Green*

Grass, Running Water – that of stories, of the narrative that alternates with the storytelling, and of the history recounted within the aforementioned narrative – are not parallel or mutually exclusive but interconnected, despite their belonging to different discursive realms. These connections allow the narrative to reach a unified point of development, which is also matched by the internal consistency and maturation of its characters. Thus, one does not get the sense that 'all of it becomes disnarrated' (Prince 303), if the hypothetical aspect of the disnarrated is meant to throw the very idea of reality into crisis. In *Green Grass, Running Water*, things are often disorienting but rarely disturbing, and traces of linearity are compatible with circularity. The circular aspect is especially evident in the ending, which carries the seeds of yet another retelling. The last line of the novel – 'And here's how it happened' (469) – is a direct echo of one of the I-narrator's early lines. At the very beginning, these words frame the entire narrative as an elaboration in reference to the past. When the line recurs at the end, it does not threaten the authenticity of the narrative but conveys the rhythmically repetitive nature of time as conceived by King. Although refrains involve an order of their own, this dance-like order comes across as preferable to the demands of a staunchly chronological trajectory.

It is impossible to make such a comment on time without attempting to understand King's indigenous world view, and its importance to his literary project. In fact, it could be said that the study of cultural influence on narrative is in keeping with Prince's vision for disnarration as expressed towards the end of his essay, where he links it to the 'pragmatics-oriented enterprise'(Prince 304) of 'modern narratology' (303). Without elaborating on the specific connotations of 'pragmatics', Prince informs us that it involves the increasing interest in 'communicative contexts' (303), and in viewing narrative as 'a situation bound transaction between two parties' (304). Since Prince's comments on pragmatics indicate an early stage of a critical approach, it might be useful to go further and explore the critical material already available on the subject of King's narrative strategy and its ideological implications. *Green Grass, Running Water* was published only five years after 'The Disnarrated', but it is more contemporary criticism that has put the spotlight on non-canonical texts such as King's, whether the focus be on form or politics.

Green Grass, Running Water is often referred to as a postmodern text, and it certainly does display multiple features associated with the genre, such as polyvocality, nonlinear temporality, metanarrative and variations on a theme. Writers such as Linda Hutcheon have written convincingly on the importance of postmodern fiction to postcolonial projects, especially in terms of its resistance to grand narratives and hegemonic discourses ('Circling the Downspout of Empire'). Gerald Vizenor, the influential indigenous American writer says that subversive figures of oral cultures are best understood as 'a nexus of signs', functioning 'at the level of language and representation' (quoted in Smith 517), and should not be perceived according to Western humanistic and anthropomorphic discourses. While acknowledging the significance of such a position, I believe one must be cautious in associating such semiotic tools directly with postmodern criticism, as critics who follow Vizenor (Smith) have done. While it is illuminating to consider how indigenous and oral culture may lend itself to sophisticated postmodern theory, it would go against the grain of King's, and even Vizenor's project to read oral culture in the shadow of postmodernity. It is not that native orature has evolved into a written form – it remains oral and thriving and exists alongside the new literature, which itself is influenced by orality.

We may apply to King his own comments on Harry Robinson, who we are told, 'develops . . . an oral syntax that defeats readers' efforts to read the stories silently to themselves, a syntax that encourages readers to read the stories out loud' (Godzilla 186). In King's novel, the use of disnarration is steeped in oral tradition even while being at home among new literary developments. Stories that go nowhere may suggest a modern loss of faith in grand narratives, but they are also linked with the archetypal garrulous storyteller in indigenous communities, who compulsively fabricates to get out of trouble or simply for the sake of putting up a performance.[3]

In conclusion, the narrative refusals and meanderings in *Green Grass, Running Water* open up the possibility of a world with a wealth of possibilities. The creative act of storytelling is portrayed as crucial to reality, as the lines between them are blurred. The specific alternatives or suggestions dismissed at different times by the narrators are not significant in themselves but in that they represent a complex cultural heritage, fertile for storytelling but also chaotic. The power of stories is not opposed to their variability; rather, it becomes important to acknowledge that the world is infused with a plurality of meanings – some of which are in harmony, some in contestation with each other, and nearly all capable of renewal in altered form.

One of the ways in which possibility is actualised, is when the four Indians carry out their notion of '[f]ixing things' (347) by changing a minute part of history – the end of a typical Western film. In the altered version, which they produce mysteriously, the Indians win and John Wayne wanes. This scene offers a redemptive moment for all the Indians watching it, but especially for Charlie, whose father Portland actually acted in the film and up to this moment, had always been on the losing side. Portland's career as an Indian in Hollywood Westerns was fraught with problems of authenticity from the start, and eventually fizzled out as the movie scene was dominated by newer actors who were deemed more physically appropriate according to the fetishistic dictates of the movie industry. For a brief period, Charlie was driven by financial constraints to take up the role that his father started out with – that of an Indian in traditional garb, at a themed car park. The change of a movie ending may not mean much, but in this case, the Indians' non-scientific powers get past the snarls of modern technology to offer an Indian a moment of real pride. Such a mischievous and harmless piece of meddling is all that is required to give history a much-needed nudge. While King embraces such twists in the narrative, these well-defined events and their equally well-defined repercussions surreptitiously work their way into a world otherwise rife with speculations on what might have happened, what has previously happened, what usually happens, and what might repeat itself but without the assurance or constraint of an identical result. It is in such a world that tricksters and meanderers can flourish.

Notes

1. The novel itself begins with
   'So.
   In the beginning, there was nothing. Just the water.'
   The character Lone Ranger appears on page 8 of the novel. After a series of interruptions from his companions, Ishmael, Robinson Crusoe and Hawkeye, The Lone Ranger tries four opening lines, each of which is rejected by his audience. The four lines are: 'Once upon a time . . . ', 'A long time ago in a faraway land...', 'Many moons comechuka... hahahahahahahahahahaha' (which is based on the phrase 'many moons have come and gone', used commonly in mildly varying forms by indigenous Americans) and 'In the beginning, God created the heaven and the earth.'
2. I have used the term 'Indian' recurrently through this essay despite its replacement by newer, preferred terms, since the former is used in the novel itself.
3. Such characters also appear in King's novel, *Medicine River*, and presumably others but unfortunately I do not have access to the rest.

WORKS CITED

Bakhtin, Mikhail. 'The Epic and the Novel.' *The Dialogic Imagination*. Ed. Michael Holquist. Austin: U of Texas P, 1981. 3–40. Print.

Hutcheon, Linda. ' "Circling the Downspout of Empire": Post-colonialism and Postmodernism.' *TSpace*. Web. 12 Dec. 2014. <http://hdl.handle.net/1807/10262>

King, Thomas. *Green Grass, Running Water*. New York: Houghton Mifflin, 1993. Print.

———.'Godzilla Vs. Postcolonial.' Web. 18 Feb. 2013. <http://pennersf.files.wordpress.com/2010/10/godzilla-complete.pdf>.

———.*Medicine River*. Canada: Penguin, 1995. Print.

———.*The 2003 CBC Massey Lectures. 'The Truth About Stories: A Native Narrative.'* Web. 18 Feb. 2013. <http://www.cbc.ca/ideas/massey-archives/2003/11/07/massey-lectures-2003-the-truth-about-stories-a-native-narrative/>.

Prince, Gerald. 'The Disnarrated.' *Narrative Theory: Critical Concepts in Literary and Cultural Studies*. Vol 1. Ed. Mieke Bal. 2004. London: Routledge, 2007. 297–305. Print.

Smith, Carlton. 'Coyote, Contingency, and Community: Thomas King's *Green Grass, Running Water* and Postmodern Trickster.' *American Indian Quarterly* 21.3 (1997): 515–34. Web. 23 Sept. 2012. <http://www.jstor.org/stable/1185521>.

Disnarration and Disability

Exploring Narrative and Corporeal Logics

Vinita Singh

The liberal humanist perspective about a direct and *neat* narrative logic in a text has been so much abused and critiqued by scholars that there has been a *severe* attention to understand the contribution of the *illogical* in/to a narrative in contemporary times. The negotiation of the narrative logic by the principle of disnarration is both complex and crucial to explore. Disnarration serves as a literary device where the narrator withholds the consequences that might have been possible and are equally *logical* which often punctures the readers' obvious or *wild* speculations about the course of a narrative. Disnarration is, most certainly, etymologically non-equivalent to what is meant by *illogical*. Nonetheless, the exploration of multiple logics that are equally potent is central to it. A reader of the disnarrated may either accept the author's logic or s/he may refute the author's reason as only one among several possible outcomes and imagine several.

This paper tries to explore the potential implied by disnarration in order to discuss its relevance to study the experiences of the disabled in three films of desire. The paper discusses how, on the one hand, the inclusion of the unwritten yet potentially possible disnarrated in these three cinematic narratives insists that one goes beyond the whole idea of a bound narrative – an extension of the Derridean text – nonetheless, on the other, it problematically builds itself upon a notion of able-ism which should be questioned and challenged. The paper thus explores the problems involved in bringing disnarration as a structural principle and disability as a bodily reality in dialectic in three cinematic narratives. The paper is also drawn by the impetus to tap the possibilities of using disnarration as a strategy to speculate multiple logics for a text in order to understand disability that defies the presumed *logic* of the normative body.

Disnarration includes 'all the events that *do not* happen though they could have and are nonetheless referred to (in a negative or hypothetical mode) by the narrative text' (Prince 30; italics original). The close examination of events that do not occur in a story, but could have reveals the versatility of the disnarrated 'as a structuring principle,' its relevance 'as a characterization device', its functions to 'thwart narrative closure'; or its functions 'to prepare and effect closure' (Baker 272)[1]. In addition to providing structure, and assuring 'thematic coherence' (274), disnarration also signals 'psychological complexity' (275).

Now, a few questions come to mind. Why would some events not take place in a narrative? But more interesting than that is the question, if the disnarrated is the path chosen not to be adopted by the text, why will it be *remembered* in 'negative or hypothetical mode'(Prince 30)? That the disnarrated is either *explicitly* remembered by the narrator or the characters in a text or inferable from the visual or textual cues for readers to refer to and imagine implies that unlike the unnarratable, the disnarrated is 'worth narrating' (Baker 272) and worth remembering.

Baker notes in the article mentioned above how examples of disnarration often include the characters looking back in time and noting what did not take place. She mentions the critical discrepancy, when the reference is to the future, between what was asserted to be certain to happen and what actually happened when it is identified at a later point in the narrative (276). Given this, although the scope of the term disnarration is inconveniently wide, ranging from explicit denials to passages of imagined or otherwise hypothetical events, it can be safely assumed that it is the *time and again* remembrance by the text of all that was possible but did not happen which differentiates the disnarrated from the 'frontal and lateral ellipses found in the narrative' which are chosen not to be remembered and recounted, which are not 'worth narrating' (272).

Where the important use of disnarration as a structural principle has been often analysed by critics, fewer attempts have been undertaken to explore this constant *stress* on *remembrance* that disnarration implies, and its implication for the character's physical and psychological dis/abilities. Other than the question of *who* in the text remembers what could have happened but did not and *what* is remembered by her or him, the question that is central to this paper is what physical or mental faculties are taken for granted or ignored which make remembrance possible by a character in the first place. Is remembrance a physical activity? Is it a mental activity? Is remembrance independent of the physical bodily constraints? Through an analysis of three films of desire, this paper explores precisely this question about how a cinematic narrative culturally constructs an *able-bodied* subject who is deemed *fit* to remember all that did not happen but could have in a narrative. The choice of a *suitable* subject who can and who is *accepted* as remembering something that didn't happen but could have is uniquely decided by the discourse within which the narrative occurs.

Re-reading Foucault from disability studies perspective illustrates this point. Foucault describes the ritual of confession in modern societies that originated in 'the long history of the Christian and juridical confession' (70). He argues that the truth about sex has to be a list of aberrations in a body that looks *like* the normal body to evoke similarity. Was it because the disabled body ruptured this project of evoking similarity that he never theorised physical disabilities in his confession science about sex? Also, by picking confession as *the* ritual that produced the discourse about sex, he presumed an able-bodied confessor – one who had the *sound* physical ability to sit on the floor, and fold her/his legs, or one who had *working* legs to come to the court and speak, or one who had the hands to write or who had the anatomical abilities to speak. This makes apparent how he focuses on confession as a symbolic act and does not interrogate the physical *conditions* of the confessor that make confessions possible.

Also implicit in the popularity and importance of confession reports is the presence of an audience to whom the confession is being made – who wants to know the truth about the confessor's sexual desires, who has the power to categorise, stigmatise or punish the confessor and who must be *pleased* by the confession. This desire for acknowledgement of deviations, passing of judgement, formation of knowledge by this second party – which might be a single person, a group of persons, an institution or the whole society – also leads to production of certain *types* of desiring subjects who are deemed *fit* to be confessing and in whose confession people will be *interested*.

Was it because the disabled bodies did not evoke similarity to those who listened to the confessions that the whole project of finding the truth about/of sex became disabled-exclusive? Was it because the disabled body ruptured the image of an ideal confessor that disability and sexuality became an off-topic – not only something which is never discussed, but also something which is never understood to exist in the first place? Is it because of this telling absence of the physically disabled from the historical project of finding truth about sexualities that the presumption – persons labelled unfit to be a part of the ritual of confession have nothing to confess about – is only rarely challenged? Rosemarie Garland Thompson has rightly remarked that absence of disability from the archive maintains the mystery around the disabled body.[2]

That a narrative of confession chooses its suitable confessor who remembers her/his sexual past and present, clarifies the point about remembrance being a political act within a cinematic narrative rife with ideological tensions. The paper argues that the way a narrative consciously chooses its subjects – who will recount those choices that were not made but could or should have been made – reveals similar narrative politics where only a few subjects are allowed to remember what the narrative situation could have been but is not. It is my contention in this paper that having the narrative privilege of remembering and reflecting upon what could have happened but did not becomes a political assertion of not only a character's identity but also of her/his physical and mental abilities and corporeal suitability.

A similar project of unearthing such politics of speech and silence within a narrative has been the central aim of the feminist narratologists and queer cultural theorists who have made revolutionary interventions focusing on marginal gendered or sexual identities. However, their interventions in the narratorial body politics with regard to corporeal alterity have been problematically less radical. For example, when carelessly applied to the study of the disabled, the feminist attempts to recognise, acknowledge and then attempt to remove the suffering that women face under the patriarchal system could imply that the suffering of one's body is always only *externally* created and is *never* a bodily reality. Such an understanding about removal of *suffering* for *emancipation* could also come to mean that any sort of suffering should be removed at any cost in order to bring freedom, normalcy and well-being to those who are *suffering*. But what is 'suffering'? Is disability a 'suffering' which must be removed in order to 'normalise' the disabled?

Carelessly borrowing this feminist understanding about oppression of women to understand all *kinds* of 'suffering' in the narrative without complicating what constitutes the feminist understanding of well-being will not only remain a half-way politics, it will also fail to challenge the notion of the disabled as 'suffering' bodies.

Even in commonsensical terms, to compare what someone's life would have been had s/he taken the path that s/he thought s/he would at a particular narrative moment but did not with what her/his life is now, at present – one needs a *working* memory. In the narrative, that means the character should be able to remember everything. Now, what ensures that that memory is reliable? Through an analysis of three films this paper will make explicit the able-bodied bodily premise of *working* memory which makes disnarration textually possible in these cinematic narratives in the first place. This stress on *working* memory that disnarration implies has huge implication for disability studies and needs to be explored.

Having laid the theoretical premise regarding the absence of the disabled body from the traditional cinematic narratives or from feminist interventions on the mainstream narratives, let me now turn to analyse individual cinematic texts to exemplify my argument about the use of disnarration and its marginalising the disabled. The examples of the disnarrated in these films of desire consist of specific references not only to what didn't happen but could have, but also to how one could have felt but didn't, and to what might have been the situation but wasn't.

In the film *Barfi*[3] the disabled protagonist, Barfi, falls in love with a girl Shruti Ghosh (played by Ileana D'cruz), who later rejects him. The story then depicts how Barfi is forced to fake a kidnapping of Jhilmil to procure 7000 rupees for his father's operation. However, as Barfi and Jhilmil have also been childhood friends, both of them start loving each other's company and fall in love with each other. The film ends with Barfi's death and Shruti recalling how Barfi and Jhilmil got married and were actually true lovers unlike Shruti herself and her husband Ranjit Sengupta.

Let us see how and for what purposes disnarration has been used in this film. The first example of the disnarrated occurs early in the story when we are informed by Shruti how she always desired to have a death like Barfi and Jhilmil – living together and then dying together – which obviously wasn't the case with her marriage. As the story unfolds, we have another example of disnarration when Shruti tells the audience how she had an affair with Barfi in Darjeeling when her father was posted there. She describes how, convinced by her mother's disnarration,[4] she opted for an able-bodied Ranjit over Barfi and how she was sad over having made such a decision. She imagines what would have happened if she had accepted Barfi's proposal. Her imagination is nostalgic for, obviously, her present married life was unhappy and unsuccessful. A third example of disnarration takes place when the police inspector recalls how he thought Barfi could have kidnapped Jhilmil but later found out it didn't happen so. Another example of disnarration happens when Shruti leaves her husband's place to go back to Barfi with an obvious desire of reclaiming her relationship with him. Given Barfi's soft corner for Shruti, the narrative appears to suggest that both of them will chart out a new journey altogether. However, such a closure is thwarted by the narrative with Barfi constantly trying to find clues to reach Jhilmil in which he ultimately succeeds and the narrative ends with Shruti as lonely as before.

In this story, the disnarrated functions both 'to provide thematic coherence – what doesn't happen appears repeatedly to be more important than what does happen – and also to thwart closure' (Baker 274). And through these episodes of disnarration, the narrative makes a subtle point that one should always pay heed to 'real' love over other material considerations. The disnarrated is the critical vehicle used to impart this message.

The film is revolutionary in the sense that it offers two disabled characters as potential sexual partners which has been only rarely attempted in Hindi cinema. However, it is interesting to note that both the persons recalling past decisions and situations that weren't actualised are able-bodied characters. They remember not only what happened to them[5] but also what happened to Barfi and Jhilmil – both disabled. At the same time, there is not even one instance in the narrative when either Barfi or Jhilmil recall what their past was like or how better/worse/ simply different their present could have been, etc. Not only does the narrative never tell us what Barfi thought or how Jhilmil experienced events, but their experiences are also always narrated and recounted by the able-bodied characters – primarily by Shruti and secondarily by the police inspector, sometimes by Jhilmil's caretaker Daaju, or a female staff member from *Muskaan*, etc.

The politics behind such mediation, which I will call, for lack of a better term, *politicised* memory, by the able-bodied character becomes yet more evident when we pay attention to the erasure of the sexual experiences of Barfi and Jhilmil in Shruti's disnarration. Although Shruti recalls her and Barfi's erotic kiss, there is no indication in her narrative of sexual desires/relationship between Barfi and Jhilmil although they too fall in love with each other much like Shruti and Barfi did. This erasure becomes yet more revealing when we focus on the abrupt cutting short of Jhilmil's extremely short flirtation with the desire to flaunt her exposed belly like Shruti or other sari-clad married women around her. Not only is Barfi's sexuality completely muted, but Jhilmil's sexual desires and fantasies are never even once mentioned. While there are incidents of physical passion between Shruti and Barfi, Jhilmil and Barfi's relationship is sublimated into a *higher* and *pure* feeling of love, care and compassion completely devoid of *the sexual*.

This erasure of the sexual experiences of the disabled body, as revealed through the various ways disnarration is employed in this narrative, poses many other larger questions. For example, what other sexual possibilities could have been equally potential had the narrative taken the alternative path to the one currently taken? Or, why have disability and sexuality been less theorised in dialectic or theorised negatively in the mainstream Bollywood cinematic narratives in general? Is it because the events of the past are all recalled by the able-bodied characters, that the sexual experiences of the disabled body are omitted in this film? How different would the narration have been had the disabled characters voiced the desires they wanted to pursue but could not? What are the reasons behind negative theorisations of disability vis-à-vis sexuality and likewise cultural representations? What have been the historical conditions that have produced and made these discourses about the disabled body acceptable? What makes the production of asexuality or hyper sexuality vis-à-vis the disabled body possible and popular? *How* can we theorise sexuality and disability together in dialectic?

Similar able-ist politics is evident in *Paa*[6] where it is Auro's mother, Vidya, who remembers how different her past could have been had she and her lover Amol not broken up. This disnarration shows very specifically how Auro was diagnosed with progeria, how Amol asks Vidya to abort the child, how Vidya refuses, breaks up with him and convinces her mother about not terminating her pregnancy, and how she copes with raising a disabled child. But none of the reminiscences describe Auro's feelings towards his disability; there is no indication on how Auro felt about his body or others around him as he grew up. We simply don't know whether Auro ever imagines what his life would have been had he not been afflicted with progeria. The narrative also doesn't develop the school-life crush of Auro's friend on Auro and instead cuts it abruptly without anyone remembering it ever again.

Yet another form of narrative politics is revealed through the examples of the use of the disnarrated in the film *Black*[7], where the protagonist Michelle is a blind girl whose letter that she has written to one of her teachers and her remembrance of her past constitutes the entire narrative.

There are several examples of disnarration in the film. One such episode of disnarration occurs when what could have happened but didn't happen before actually does happen – when, for eleven times, Michelle thinks she would pass her BA exam which she doesn't until her twelfth attempt. This is a reference to what supposedly will happen and does indeed turn out not to happen, at least not the eleven times. This kind of disnarration has been termed by Baker as 'proleptic disnarration – a kind of disnarration that becomes apparent at a later point in time in the story' (276).

The recalling and remembrance by Michelle herself of the sexual desires that she felt for her teacher Desai but couldn't pursue, and then, Desai – who is not given an opportunity to recall his past at all – suffering from Alzheimer's which is a mental disease not disability, may seem to challenge the argument that the paper has been making this far about the able-bodied bodily premise underlying disnarration in these films. However, it is important to note that the only reason Michelle – a visually disabled girl – could be the narrator of her own experiences is because her physical deformity hasn't had an impact over her *working* memory. Also, her *working* memory is privileged only when she has *defeated* her physical deformity by passing her BA exam in her twelfth attempt. That the narrative relies upon Michelle's memory over Desai's memory – which is rejected as faltering because of his mental disease – only when she has *controlled* her physical limitations, reveals yet again how this narrative is embedded in the cultural matrix of able-ism.

A close examination of all these stories shows that in these films something which might happen but doesn't happen is remembered only by the able-bodied characters and that has a huge implication for the disabled body.

Urvashi Butalia says that at the level of popular memory, the India–Pakistan partition overshadows the importance of independence because of its much more *direct* impact on the lives of people (91). While the word *direct* obviously evokes the memories of forced migration and sense of loss (of family, friends, soil and community) that people on both sides of the border experienced, the reference to *material* impact on the *physical* bodies cannot be ignored either.

Taking a cue from Butalia's statement I have tried in this paper to build my argument about 'narrative corporeality' (Punday 86) and its role in the events of disnarration. To give an example, while feminist interventions have made possible the production of texts – both written and cinematic – that represent the memories of partition as experienced by women in order to critique the male-centric recorded nationalist history, fewer attempts have been undertaken to understand the ways this project produced narratives with a standardised image of the heroic/tragic body of a woman – a woman who, by virtue of her *sound* physical and mental health, has the strength to fight or who suffered due to her gendered identity and whose corporeal otherness contributed absolutely in non-significant ways.

That these narratives of partition have only rarely tried to explore memories of the disabled women – women who became physically impaired during the violent attacks that took place, or women who became mentally ill because they could not come to terms with the trauma of partition, or women who were already physically/mentally impaired and had to undergo the whole experience of partition evokes once again how a *healthy* and *able-bodied* bodily premise is stressed for a memory that can be trusted.

Through an analysis of examples of disnarration from three cinematic texts, I have tried to point to the strong manipulative effects it can have, turning seemingly objective narration into an overly biased one. As disnarration refers to those events that could have happened but did not, it also implies what should be the *ideal* in a particular situation or for a particular person or group. Disnarration thus also serves as a narrative device that renders socio-cultural norms visible and opens them to be debated. Therefore its contribution in opening the debate about marginalisation of the disabled even in an apparently reliable narrative cannot be ignored.

Through this paper I have not only tried to question the premise that fails to interrogate the absence of the lived experience of the disabled bodies from most of the episodes of disnarration in various cinematic narratives but also how its inclusion will enable us to nuance beliefs within narratology that are taken for granted and go unquestioned. An equally valid and important point regarding the use of disnarration in the cinematic narratives is that the refusal of narrative closure that disnarration implies strongly suggests the role of the audience's imagination in treating the *author-willed* narrative closures as culture-bound and temporary. By rendering what we understand by corporeal logic of a normative human body visible, the disnarrated in these films also stresses to look at corporeal difference not in terms of deficiency but as one among *several possible and yet potent* selfhoods.

Notes

1. While analysing France's first novella collection *Les Cent Nouvelles Nouvelles* (c. 1462), Mary J. Baker in 'The "Disnarrated" in *Les Cent Nouvelles Nouvelles*' describes the various uses of disnarration in tale no. 77 and no. 81.
2. Rosemarie Garland Thompson, in 'Integrating Disability: Transforming Feminist Theory', describes how the archive determines what we can know. She says: ' . . . there has been no archive, no template for understanding disability as a category of analysis and knowledge, as a cultural trope, and an historical community. So just as the now widely recognized centrality of gender and race analyses to all knowledge was unthinkable thirty years ago, disability is still not an icon on many critical desktops' (74).
3. The film was directed by Anurag Basu and released in September 2012. It was a major box-office hit, gaining accolades and critical acclamation both in India and abroad. The film, which also got nominated for Oscars from India, is a story of a man called Barfi Johnson (played by Ranbir Kapoor) and Jhilmil Chatterjee (played by Priyanka Chopra) – both deaf and dumb by birth.
4. In the film, Shruti, having fallen in love with Barfi, expresses their mutual desire to get married to her parents. Getting to know about Shruti's decision, her mother discloses to her how she (Shruti's mother) almost ran away with her lover in her youth only to change her mind, and then married Shruti's father for practical reasons.
5. For example, Shruti remembers how she chose Ranjit when half of the college girls were crazy about him and the police inspector remembers how his waist size reduced from 50 to 40 inches.
6. The film was directed by R. Balki and released in December 2009. It narrates the story of Auro (played by Amitabh Bachchan) who has progeria, his mother Vidya (played by Vidya Balan) and his father Amol Atre (played by Abhishek Bachchan).
7. The film was directed by Sanjay Leela Bhansali and released in February 2005. It narrates the journey of a blind girl Michelle

(played by Rani Mukherjee) from her childhood to her youth and later and Desai, her teacher (played by Amitabh Bachchan), who is diagnosed with Alzheimer's.

WORKS CITED

Baker, Mary J. 'The "Disnarrated" in *Les Cent Nouvelles Nouvelles.*' *Orbis Litterarum* 50.5(1995): 272–77. Web. 27 February 2013.

Butalia, Urvashi. 'Abducted and Widowed Women: Questions of Sexuality and Citizenship during Partition.' In *Embodiment: Essays on Gender and Identity*, ed. Meenakshi Thapan. 1997: 91–106. Web. 12 January 2013. <http://jan.ucc.nau.edu/~sj6/butaliaabductedwomen.pdf>.

Foucault, Michel. *The History of Sexuality*. Vol. 1.Trans. Robert Hurley. New York: Pantheon Books, 1978. Web. 27 February 2013.

Prince, Gerald. *Narrative as Theme: Studies in French Fiction.* USA: U of Nebraska P, 1992. Web. 28 February 2013.

Punday, Daniel. *Narrative Bodies: Toward a Corporeal Narratology*. New York: Palgrave Macmillan, 2003. Web. 28 February 2013.

Thompson, Rosemarie Garland. 'Integrating Disability: Transforming Feminist Theory.' *Centro de Estudos Sociais Laboratorio Associado, Universidade de Coimbra, Intimidade Projectos*. 73–103. Web. 9 December 2012. <http://www.ces.uc.pt/projectos/intimidade/media/Integrating%20Disability,%20Transforming%20Feminist%20Theory.pdf>

Do these Ruins Narrate our Pasts?

An Examination of W.G. Sebald's Narratives

Krishnan Unni. P

The discourse of disnarration, more than the textual and intervening strategies involved in it, proposes a whole range of questions connected to the ways of looking at, explicating and carrying out alternate reading of texts in our time. Having understood the metafictional aspects of postmodern texts, the disnarration in them offers the possibilities of subversion and an opportunity of submerging more than a language game they provide; but a departure from the panoramic and diegetic aspects of what the language stands for, and hence, the question of the plurality of worlds figuring in them assumes specific importance. When Gerald Prince insisted on the metafictionality and open-endedness of modernist fictions that 'foreground the production of a world by language, the fact that the novel [. . .] is a statement about novels and the writing of novels' (Prince 7), the intertextual and non-linear features of the texts come into focus very much. No text escapes from the mechanisms of the confluence centered on non-linear and asymmetrical narration. More than the negation of closure, these texts primarily opened up the importance of multiple ways of looking at the fixed pattern of reading the narrated incidents, occurrences, phenomena of locating reader-responses and the methodology of re-articulating the content along the lines of a set of meanings.

The narrative jumblings and the counter-contextual interpolations in the texts of Georges Perec, John Fowles, Thomas Pynchon, Carlos Fuentes, Diamela Eltit and Bernard Cohen are some good examples of this. Disnarration appears in the postmodern texts as a means of subverting the fixed genres of textual fixations and appropriating the unsaid or rather the un-narrated events, sights and instances. This feature of disnarration definitely marks a turning point in the history of reading contemporary texts, and more deviant ways of understanding the past in the context of contemporaneity become important. Moreover, disnarrated texts with their ruptures and fissures pose questions of all full-flooded narratives and point to the need to find discontinuities in them. Seen in this context, one major problem that arises seems to be the end of a set pattern of reading or words. The reading of disnarrated texts is a digression from the plain understanding of any narrative and it involves the contradictory and incriminating features of explicating meanings. This paper will look at W.G. Sebald's texts in the light of the several pasts and histories involved in the textual construction and the ruins of many pasts, cultures and nations that function as the bedrock of these narratives.

Ruins are intricately connected to the modern and postmodern discourses of architecture, literature, art, music and other areas of social sciences and human investigation. In the texts of W.G. Sebald, ruins often resurface as the product of contemporary times, while very little attention is given to them in practical life. They are either neglected or sidelined as spaces/places of pasts, not worth studying. The engagement of Sebald's themes with ruins is connected to the geographical dissimilarity, writings of war times, postcards, stamps, photographs, narratives of war-torn Europe, the search of the historian/narrator for validity of truth, claims of the government upon verifying the facts, registers and scrap books, and other areas of investigation.

The complex and tightly woven compendium of Sebald's texts, therefore, partakes both of modern and postmodern anxieties that make them part of our contemporaneity, which is paradigmatically redefined. The difficulty in preserving and retaining the ruins in our times is the main challenge against narration and this, in all its tenacity gives rise to disnarration in literatures. However, it should be noted that this disnarration is not anti-narration as this has a definite standpoint of making what is narrated heard. The texts are straddled with uneven mechanisms for creating alternate worlds, language and situations. Sebald's texts articulate in the mode of self-critiquing what is narrated and this involvement of his characters, situations and events makes up the new phase of disnarration far beyond the disnarrated language we have encountered with modern Western literatures.

In his article 'Authentic Ruins', Andreas Huyssen writes:

> Authentic ruins, at least as they have existed in the eighteenth and nineteenth centuries seem to have no place in late capitalism's culture of commodity and memory. Commodities in general do not age well. They become obsolete and are thrown out or recycled. Buildings are thrown out or destroyed. The chance for things to age and to become ruins has diminished, ironically in the same measure that the average age of the populace continues to rise. (19)

Huyssen's observations are particularly important to make an entry into Sebald's texts as his statement examines the two sides of the global city and the destruction wrought upon architecture, offices and roads. Moreover, this statement clearly indicates the deviant ways of the working of the capital and the consequent elision of memory, particularly in post-war Europe, where ageing of the structures is well replaced by global recycling and alternate constructions.

While modern European cultures were interested in their own way to claim the ruins of the past, the postmodern culture, it seems, recycles everything by building up huge pantheons etc. by discarding the old. This mismatch inherent in Western civilisation needs to be clearly oriented in connection with our experience with the past. The dichotomy of the modern subject as a product of the ruins and the postmodern subject as witness seems to be the pretext upon which the discourse of the un-narrated past of Europe is organised.

The authenticity of ruins has become a big question in our time as we have many notions of the past lurking within us. For Sebald, the relationship with ruins is one of constant deferment and distancing. The claims of authenticity, as his texts imply, are the reorientation of the past through the modes of journeying, by arraying memories of distant past and the reported narratives, in which the protagonists of the texts undertake the tough task of inventing a 'present' interspersed with sights and significant tell-tale signs. Ruins are the constant citations of Sebald's protagonists.

Walter Benjamin, in his postulation of the angel of history, codifies what is embedded as 'ruin gazing' (184). Benjamin's angel of history is not a narrator, but a disnarrator, since it involves itself in the perverse mechanism of turning toward the past that is speedily vanishing and looking toward the future in which the elements of what is witnessed become suspect. The allegory of this angel of history is the difficult condition of the human in the twentieth century as s/he is devoid of a past of absolute recollection. In Benjamin's attempts to recapture a sense of history, this angel, as Hannah Arendt implies, creates 'a shock of experience' (Arendt 1) for the aestheticisation of ruins. Benjamin's theory of history contains this aestheticisation of ruins though he extends the role of history into the cultural and political dimensions of his times. The snippets of history and observation of the past of collapse and ruins, it seems, is an act of investing in the present the methodology to create multiple presents for further introspection. It becomes clear that Benjamin's thoughts have deeply influenced Sebald in his construction of narratives that may seem like travel writing where protagonists encounter fixed locations with multidimensional aspects of the past and polyvalent structures of the present that both negate and affirm their experiences in the past.

The interloping narratives of Sebald create a possibility of disnarration by disengaging with fixed meanings, meanderings and memory – in other words, themes related to the usual narration and connection with the past. Unlike the philosophic texture of Benjamin, Sebald breaks up the narration by his careful crafting of different tropes of memory and the inculcation of the archival material, which were previously not archived in museums and libraries. While memory for Sebald is the prime source of constructing the narrative, the sights, sounds and smells that make up the events and situations of history seem to offer the possibility of constructing the counter-archive that never can be examined further for claiming the validity of essence and truth. Sebald disorganises the narratives and creates several counter-narratives. The counter-narratives oppose the streamlined narrative plan of his texts and offer possibilities of generating discourses of dissimilar nature. The web of uncertainty, thus created, is very much a model of disnarration.

Any attempt to disnarrate or anti-narrate is impossible without juggling with the various innuendoes of memory, which, in other words, functions as the central terrain that destabilises the act of witnessing, recording, perceiving and writing. Sebald encounters several tropes of memory from modern literatures and postmodern narratives in his texts. However, he refuses to follow a simple pattern of adherence to one feature of narration. In *Matter and Memory*, Henrik Bergson distinguishes two types of memory: the voluntary memory and the involuntary memory. By comparing voluntary memory to the process of writing a lesson, Bergson writes: 'at this precise moment, I know my lesson by heart; someway it has become a memory [souvenir], that it is imprinted on my memory [la memoire]' (Bergson 79). In Bergson's terminology, voluntary memory is related to progression and repetition, a feature common in all narratives in general. The 'regressive memory' is not associated with any prolongation, but with 'recording' perpetual images (Bergson 83). This 'regressive memory' actively turns toward the past compared to 'habit memory'. European modern literature since the publication of Marcel Proust's *In Search of Lost Time* is dependent on this regressive or involuntary memory. The Proustian memory is transmuted into European modern literatures mainly through Samuel Beckett and James Joyce.

Throughout in *Matter and Memory*, Bergson defines the unconscious as impotence, perhaps a definite break from Sigmund Freud's way of looking at the unconscious as the potent form of cultivating instincts. Bergson links the extension of the consciousness to the present, to the actually lived and thus incorporates a whole terrain of experiences. The limitation of this consciousness extends the vision of existence. Existence is attributed in Bergson's terminology both to the consciousness and the unconsciousness, to a state where no lived experience is possible any longer. Since memories have an intractable relationship with time, as Gilles Deleuze comments, they are 'impassable' (1). The fact that memories never can be tied to factual conditions is the first step that marks the terrain of disnarration as any narrative in the process of absorption and representation of incidents, events, situations and contexts, may never have the 'lived' or the 'live' experience of entirety; at the same time, the language with its flippancy deceives or rather debunks the narrated. The struggle within the corpus of memory itself is another ruin of existence. As we see the ruins in our time or civilisation, the idea that memory is the ruin – but with the notion that this should necessarily precipitate our consciousness – seems to be the idea behind disnarration. In Sebald, we find disnarration approximating this feature to narrate further or to re-contextualise a troubled past in the present of constant deferring.

In the reminiscences of the narrator in *The Rings of Saturn*, Sebald complicates Bergsonian memory by invoking a system of objects indecipherable and also claiming that in the visit to Holland, he was struck with unnameable objects and events. Sebald writes:

> The reading room in Southwold is opened at every morning at seven (save only Christmas day) and remains open until almost midnight. At best it attracts a handful of visitors during the holidays, and a few who would come across the threshold leave again as they have taken a brief look around in the uncomprehending way characteristic of such holiday makers. The Reading Room is thus always deserted but for one or two surviving fishermen and seafarers sitting in silence in the armchairs, whiling the time away. (92–93)

While the narration is clear about the reading room, gradually this turns out to be the occasional forgetting when he (the narrator) talks about the 'marbled cover of the log book' searching for the 'mysterious silence of the written word' (93). Gradually, the sliding into the photographic history of the First World War by the narrator distances the histories of the fishermen from fixed places to the unimaginable histories of the places that figure in the book on war photography. The narrator says:

> There are illustrations of all conceivable forms of violent death, from the shooting down of a single aviation pioneer over the Somme estuary to the mass slaughter in the swamps of Galicia, the pictures of the French town reduced to rubble, corpses rotting in the no-man's land between the trenches, woodlands razed by artillery fire, battleships sinking under black smoke of petroleum smoke, armies on the march, never ending stream of refugees, shattered zeppelins, streams from Preszemsyl and St Quentin, from Montfaucon and Gallipoli, scenes of destruction, mutilation, starvation, conflagration and freezing cold. The

> titles are almost without exception, bitterly ironic – When cities deck their streets for war! This was a forest! This was a man! There is some corner of a Foreign Field that Forever is England. (94–95)

This description makes it clear that as in a cinematographic panning shot, the narrator investing in multiple memories loses the sense of particular fixities of places while browsing the book. The history of the fishermen provided in the text is a gateway to locate the histories of a community prior to the war. But this history, as the narrator's desperate attempts indicate, is seriously fraught with discontinuities because it slips into the uneven spatial tropes of the ruins of the present. In other words, a sense of the past is deluded by the ruins of an immediate present. The disnarrated context here is both the history of the fishermen and the partly narrated, incomplete history of the First World War.

The ruins create a sense of wonder and a desire to undertake travel in *The Rings of Saturn*. The disnarrated events further assume the form of ruins. The narrator's journey to Hamburger's house is another instance where he mixes up the past of the poet Holderlin with the present of Hamburger. The narrator asks: 'Across what distances in time do the elective affinities and correspondences connect? How is it that one perceives oneself in another human being, or, if not oneself, then one's own precursor?'(*The Rings of Saturn*, 181). These questions, it must be noted, are the nerve centres of what Sebald's narration does not offer by telling a simple story.

As the correspondences get difficult to connect, the narrative also faces dissimilarities and incomprehensible paradoxes. Paraphrasing Walter Benjamin, 'this trash of history' (209), it is clear that another level of operation of memory is highlighted – which is neither Bergsonian nor anti-Bergsonian, but one that highlights the need of imagining for the formation of memory. This can be termed 'tertiary memory' as Sebald constantly juggles with the narrative imbalances, photographs and uneven events of history.

Tertiary memory is an 'invented memory', not an actual memory nor the involuntary memory that forms the sub-text of many modern narratives. This memory suggests the need to redefine the ruins, historical occurrences and different narrative tropes. Inside Sebald's narratives, this 'tertiary memory' functions as the internal dynamism that delinks the one– to–one correspondence between one incident and another, the text and the reader, and one narrative with another narrative. Readers are prone to think of the other side or the alternate passage from the journeys of Sebaldian protagonists and parallel to what the writer narrates. The invented memory claims its existence by making the readers think about the other possibilities of the journeys and by viewing of the photographs to study the modalities of history and text. As commented by J.J. Long,

> Sebald's narrator's walking, then is deliberately, inefficient and one might say, anti–disciplinary. This tendency to explore byways rather than make beelines goes hand in hand with a narrative technique that is multiply digressive: it repeatedly shifts focus, as each narration is soon abandoned in favour of another digression or a brief return to the story of the journey itself; it frequently changes the context within which phenomena are understood, evoking a parallel, mythic temporality that transfigures the quotidian object-world and produces a split attention, a kind of distraction, in both the narrator and the reader; and it frequently gets sidetracked into lengthy enumerations of physical objects. (140)

Long's analysis clearly outlines the 'tertiary memory' as the only way by which the narratives of the ruins can be brought into focus. This digressive mechanism offers an alternative to the straddled post-war generation of Europe who cannot forget the terrible past of the holocaust. The death and destruction of the holocaust along with the ruins that are visible even in contemporary times tend to lend memory a new domain. The post-war generation tries to invent memories by re-imagining incidents and other histories parallel to the histories narrated.

At the same time, this digression is not only a quick jump from time and space; but a movement inside the narration that negates outright the fixity of all meanings and memories, and paradoxically the relevance of understanding one history based on memory, which Peter Brooks would call 'narrative desire'(27). The disnarration of Sebald optimises narrative desire by claiming the 'tertiary memory' as the tool for narrating the ruins.

In *Austerlitz*, memory struggles with archives. Archives in this text generate a number of important discourses connected to disnarration. The question of archives in this text raises a number of issues connected to disnarration: Would the archive be ever representable to viewers/readers? By what modalities can the archives of memory function? Can an archive be a reliable source of understanding our past and past situations? Looking at the complex ways of archive formation and the role of the archivist, Derrida writes: 'if we want to know what the archive meant . . . we will only know in times to come' (36). Archives, for Derrida, have certainly other dubious functions embedded in them; which make them inconspicuous for the determination of a set of contexts and pasts. Inside every archive, there are traces that are never deciphered and are perpetually deferred. The archivist 'produces more archive, and that is why the archive is never closed. It opens out on to the future' (Derrida 68). The recorded past of Austerlitz undergoes a series of changes and his present obfuscates all official forms of knowing the past. In his moorings into the library of the National Bibliotheque, Austerlitz engages in the process of constructing his troubled past, a product of disjuncture and disconnectivity. The library with the amazing collection of archives forms the alterity of Austerlitz – more precisely, it makes a space for him to dissociate from the fixed past and belonging to any fixed place. The awareness of Austerlitz that the library was built on a place which was the warehouse for the storage of goods, repair and classification shakes him and makes him realise that archives are built upon ruins.

Progressing from Derrida's arguments of the archive, Helmut Schmitz comments on Austerlitz's experience in the library: 'Erected on the site where Germans once stored their possessions they had stolen from the Parisian Jews, the monstrous building becomes the example of the progressive obliteration of the past' (294). Austerlitz's desire to produce a counter archive completely fails. Somewhere, the spectral past of the Parisian Jews haunts him; and this aspect, needless to say, functions as the best form of disnarrative in the text as the narrative disengages totally from the sight and circumstance.

The question of disnarration is further clear in a series of dialogues of Austerlitz and other characters. The fissures in Austerlitz's memory replace any modality of recollecting the past. Recollecting Elias' description of Llanwddyn, Sebald narrates:

> Llanwddyn had been particularly famous for its games of football on the village green when the full moon shone in summer, often lasting all night and played by over ten dozen youths and men of almost every age, some of them from neighbouring villages. The story of the football games in Llanwddyn occupied my imagination for a long time, said Austerlitz, first and foremost, I am sure, because Elias never told me anything else about his own life either before or afterwards. (*Austerlitz,* 51)

In this narration, Austerlitz's memory is interloped into Elias' narration and consequently his forgetting about what he told him about the place. The place is the real problematic terrain for Austerlitz as he has sporadic convulsions of memory narrating them. At the same time, he lives in each and every place, though not physically, but in his imaginative recollections and meanderings. Post-war Europe has many such places that function as the tropes of narration. The wanderer's desire to be a part of such places is fraught with contradictions. These places of ruins, more than the nostalgia and at times derision they evoke, seem to be the locations of narrative straddling. Examining Braudel's time and historical narratives, Paul Ricoeur writes:

> . . . the plurality of historical times extolled by Braudel is an expansion of the cardinal feature of narrative time, namely, its ability to combine in variable proportions the chronological component of the episode and the achronological component of the configuration. Every one of the temporal levels required by historical explanation may be seen as a duplication of this dialectic. (225)

Ricoeur's concern over the many temporalities existing together has created a historical breakthrough in the study of the historical narratives (16). Austerlitz, in his attempts to relive such temporalities, offers a vibrant genealogy of many memories colliding and his journey is more for finding people and making histories out of them. Sebald makes the follow-up of Austerlitz's Llanwddyn narration:

> This notion of mine about the subaquatic existence of the people at Llanwddyn also had something to do with the album which Elias first showed me on our return home that evening, containing several photographs of his birthplace, now sunk beneath the water. As there were no other pictures in this manse, I leafed again and again through these few photographs, which came into my own possession only much later along with the Calvinist calendar, until the people looking out of them, the blacksmith in his leather apron, Elias's father the sub-postmaster, the shepherd walking along the village street with his sheep, and most of all a girl sitting in a chair in the garden with her little dog on her lap, became familiar to me as if I were living with them down the lake. (*Austerlitz*, 52)

In this description of space, Austerlitz creates an atmosphere of how and to what extent the possibilities of multi-temporalities can act as forms of desire by negating the sense of nostalgia stationed at one place. Desire, for Austerlitz, is the product of many existences, and hence it distances any fixity with one particular place.

The inclusion of photographs in Sebald's texts raises questions of the verifiability of the narratives. The absence of the narrator in the photographs is the most distinctive feature in Sebald's narratives. Photographs deny the modalities of direct representation and problematise the way of correspondence between the viewer and the narrator. The narrated self in the photographs never shows justice to the written text as the time, space and events in the photographs connote desirability within the narrative. In other words, these photographs, as they seem to suggest, question the corpus of the narratives mainly told by the first person, who in Sebald's texts is often a wanderer in war-torn Europe or a researcher who is labelled the spokesman of a new history. The undeniable issue of his narration getting misrepresented is what is mirrored in the photographs as they seem to suggest an alternate way of looking at the sights, situations and ruins of the past.

In the background of the holocaust experience and shattered experience, Ulrich Baer comments on the Lodz ghetto, claiming that those who view it as a totalising Nazi impact have 'a simplistic understanding of the photograph as originating with an all-knowing, morally vacated, and near-demonic subject behind ghetto view finder [*sic*], someone who views absolute powers of execution and cognition over what is seen' (21). In a similar attempt, we find Sebald negating all totalising attempts of viewing the photographs in his narratives. The dispossessed and the voiceless are the ones who figure in Sebald's photographs, as the example of the photograph of Ambrose Adelwarth in *The Emigrants* (137) shows. As Adelwarth's experiences are rich and varied, the costume he has in the photographs negates his particular Arab history thrust on a particular place. The photographs of the charred skulls (*The Emigrants*, 131), and the state archives (*Austerlitz,* 144) in *Austerlitz* are two different dimensions of Austerlitz's narration of his deviant existence in post-holocaust Europe. These photographs negate the linear narration and perception and offer the possibility of personalising the archives as their representation in the texts suggests the ways of reading the interiority of the subject.

The interesting way in which the subject and the photograph function within the text makes the text an engaging platform to destabilise narrative fixities and meanings. The non-static and unstable narrative, more than a format of disnarrative, argues for some way of recognising within the jungle of the past where memories are unevenly chained. The notion of the 'metapicture' (Mitchell 57) is appropriate as Sebald's photographic images produce more production of images within them. Photographs, as the counter-narrative within the main narrative, in their asymptomatic nature, digress the recovery of the past as memories of their own ruins.

J. J. Long contends in his analysis of *Austerlitz*: 'the archive is, to a certain extent, redeemed at the text's epiphanic moment, the moment when Austerlitz finally succeeds in discovering his mother's image in the theatrical archives of Prague. Like the woman in the Thereinstadt film (whom she does not resemble), this woman also seems to tally with Austerlitz's dim memory of his mother' (161). The photographs in *Austerlitz* and in *The Emigrants* particularly help us construct a counter-current of understanding the other side of the past, as the narrative fails and the unclear memories further diminish the possibility of making any journey remembered in its fullness. The narrative failures are not really comprehended by the photographs; on the other hand, they are the substrata which digress memories as the places and spaces in Sebald's texts are open for endless discussions and ramifications.

The politics of disnarrated events in Sebald's texts in connection with the photographs and the journeying of the protagonists creates an alternative mechanism of trying to engage with many interiorities rather than looking at one particular self as the source of all narration. This aspect signifies what John Zilcosky's comment on a text like *Austerlitz* as 'postmodern crypto-bildungsroman' means (697). Zilcosky comments: 'As Sebald knew from his earlier works, getting lost contains within it the seeds of a journey "home": in the case of *Austerlitz*, toward the historical sites of the Nazi crimes' (697). The past of the ruins in Austerlitz's experience becomes the ruins of the present as these ruins can never be properly codified by memories and archives. The value of the ruins of post-war Europe is undermined here as we move toward a set of intractable questions of archaeology, memory, archives and representation. Ruins, it seems, never become the sites of wonder and phenomenal enthralling of the past. The ruins are the sites of re-configuring where we stand in connection to the many pasts given and narrated to us. The role of disnarration here is to resurface the many pasts without concentrating on individual subjectivity as this may tend to orient us toward a fixed understanding of the past.

Sebald's disnarrated texts, more than counter-narratives or anti-narratives, offer the possibility of understanding the possibilities of writing, re-presentation and reflexivity. More than the textual meanings generated, this attempts to open up a new discourse of understanding the dimensions of narrating/writing as the representation of ruins. Perhaps, this awareness, true to state a post-Blanchotian one, makes the ruins of seeing different from the ruins of narrative.

WORKS CITED

Arendt, Hannah. 'Introduction'. *Ruins of Modernity*. Ed. Hell, Julia and Andreas Schonle. Durham and London: Duke UP, 2010. 1–14. Print.

Baer, Ulrich. *Spectral Evidence: The Photography of Trauma.* Cambridge: MIT Press, 2001. Print.

Benjamin, Walter. Qtd in Julia Hell, 'Imperial Ruin Gazers, Or Why Did Scipio Weep?' In *Ruins of Modernity,* ed. Hell, Julia and Andreas Schonle. Durham and London: Duke UP, 2010. 169–92. Print.

———. Qtd in Todd Samuel Presner, 'Hegel's Philosophy of World History Via Sebald's Imaginary of Ruins'. In *Ruins of Modernity,* ed. Hell, Julia and Andreas Schonle. Durham and London: Duke UP, 2010. 193–211. Print.

Bergson, Henri. *Matter and Memory.* Trans. N. M. Paual and W. S. Palmer. New York: Zone Books, 1994. Print.

Brooks, Peter. *Reading for the Plot: Design and Intention in Narrative.* Cambridge, MA: Harvard UP, 1984. Print.

Deleuze, Gilles. Qtd in Michal Herer, 'For the (Im) Possibility of Art in Control Societies,' 1. Web.12 May 2009.<www.wuw-warsaw.pl/download/Michal Herer.pdf>

Derrida, Jacques. *The Archive Fever: A Freudian Impression.*Trans. Eric Pernowitz. Chicago and London: Chicago UP, 1996. Print.

Huyssen, Andreas. 'Authentic Ruins: Products of Modernity.' In Hell, Julia and Anderas Schonle, ed. *Ruins of Modernity.* Durham and London: Duke UP, 2010. 17–28. Print.

Long, J.J. *W.G. Sebald: Image, Archive and Modernity.* New York: Columbia UP, 2007. Print.

Mitchell, W.J.T. *Picture Theory.* Chicago: U of Chicago P, 1994. Print.

Prince, Gerald. 'The Disnarrated.' *Style* 22. 22.1 (Spring 1988): 1–8. Pennsylvania: The Pennsylvania State UP, 1988. Print.

Ricoeur, Paul. *Time and Narration.* Vol 1. Trans. Kathleen MacLaughlin and David Pellauer. Chicago and London: The U of Chicago P, 1984. Print.

Schultz, Helmut. ' "[. . .] Only Signs Everywhere of the Annihilation" – W.G. Sebald's *Austerlitz.' On their Own Terms: The*

Legacy of National Socialism in Post-1990 German Fiction. The New Germany in Context. Birmingham: Birmingham UP, 2004. 297–98. Print.

Sebald, W.G. *Austerlitz*. Trans. Anthea Bell. New York: The Modern Library, 2001.Print.

———. *The Emigrants*. Trans. Michael Hulse. London: The Harvill Press, 1996.Print.

———. *The Rings of Saturn*. Trans. Michael Hulse. London: Vintage, 2002. Print.

Zilcosky, John. 'Lost and Found: Disorientation, Nostalgia and Holocaust Melodrama in Sebald's *Austerlitz*'. *MLN* 121.3 (2006): 687–99. Print.

Marketing Democracy to a Dictatorship

Pablo Larraín's *No* and the Pragmatics of National Narratives

NISHA VISWANATHAN

In the months of September and October 1988, the fifteen-year-old gag on Chile was lifted for the first time since Augusto Pinochet seized power post the military coup in 1973 that overthrew Salvador Allende's socialist government. Succumbing to international pressure to legitimise his government, Pinochet called for a national referendum in 1988 to determine whether he should continue as President for another eight years, or step down and make way for democracy in Chile[1]. The people of Chile could vote either 'Yes' or 'No' to eight more years under Pinochet. Every night for twenty-seven nights leading up to the day of the referendum, fifteen minutes of airtime on national television were allotted to the YES and NO camps to make their respective cases. Many Chileans believed that the outcome of the referendum would be manipulated in favour of the government and were, therefore, surprised by the triumph of the NO faction which led to the deposing of Pinochet.

The NO campaign, which emerged victorious against all odds, remains one of the few successful attempts in history to terminate a dictatorship non-violently. Besides being crippled by the absence of a candidate to promote, the NO campaign was burdened with the task of making the negative appeal to the public. Chilean film-maker Pablo Larraín's film *No* (2012) gives a fictionalised account of the making of the historical advertising campaign by the NO camp and explores its contribution to the termination of Pinochet's brutal totalitarian regime[2]. The film details three prominent attempts at imagining and narrativising Chile as a nation in the months leading up to the plebiscite – the narrative propagated by the YES camp and the two conflicting narratives of Chile that initially divided the NO coalition into two factions and vied for its unanimous acceptance. The YES campaign conceptualised a Chile defined by the economic progress wrought by the neoliberal reforms introduced by Pinochet, while promoting the dictator in the guise of a benign, 'civilian' president. The NO faction displayed a chaotic front in the beginning[3]. Not only did many members of the NO faction doubt the authenticity of the 1988 plebiscite, they also believed that by participating in it, they would be legitimising the fraudulent 1980 constitution that mandated it. The majority of the coalition thus considered their options to be limited to 'rais[ing] awareness' regarding Pinochet's many human rights violations and thereby 'fill[ing] the spaces the dictatorship had to open . . .' (*No*). But, the creative heads of the campaign Eugenio Gracia and José Manuel Salcedo (of whom René Saavedra, the protagonist of the film, is an amalgamation) opt for a fantastic depiction of a Chile yet to be born, where jubilant citizens are out on the streets dancing and singing of the happiness that is on its way to their country.

This paper reads *No* as a battle between diverse, often contradictory, televisual narratives of Chile for dominance over the national imagination in the weeks preceding the referendum. In the light of the narrative trajectory conventionally adopted by national narratives wherein the historicity of the nation is strongly emphasised, the NO campaign's rejection of Chile's factual past in favour of an imagined future as the basis for narrativising a Chile on the cusp of democracy presents a fascinating departure. This paper carefully examines the conflict within the NO coalition over which national narrative to champion via the NO campaign. Using a relevance-theoretic approach, it analyses the effectiveness of the counterintuitive[4] national narrative that is eventually disseminated through the NO polispots[5] over the anti-Pinochet narrative that the NO campaign proposed to promote in its earlier stages. In doing so, it hopes to delineate some implications of the NO faction's choice to disseminate an ahistorical national narrative with the hopes of mobilising public demand for a new national mood.

Nation and Commemoration

The notion of 'nation', defined by Benedict Anderson as 'an imagined political community' (6), depends for its perpetuation on the concealment of its constructedness. The reification of 'nation' is therefore considerably dependent on acts of narrativisation. Though the emplotment of national narratives mandates that its temporal contours appear vague[6] and that its emergence be shrouded in mystery, the 'nation' paradoxically relies on a sense of certainty accorded by the shared memory of an immediate past. Acts of memorialisation and commemoration are considered essential for the fortification of national identities. Since nations have 'no clearly identifiable births', Anderson argues that they can only be narrativised backwards, 'start[ing] from an originary present', in a 'curious inversion of conventional genealogy' (205). Narratives thus fashioned are invariably 'marked by deaths':

> Yet the deaths that structure the nation's biography are of a special kind . . . the nation's biography snatches, against the going mortality rate, exemplary suicides, poignant martyrdoms, assassinations, executions, wars, and holocausts. But, to serve the narrative purpose, these violent deaths must be remembered/forgotten as 'our own'. (Anderson 205–6)

Taking into account the importance of the act of remembering to the project of nation building, Urrutia, the film's fictional counterpart to the head of the NO coalition, argues for the utilisation of the campaign as a medium to underscore: '[the] human rights [abuses], exile, injustice, arbitrary arrests, torture, disappearances. All the pain we've lived through. We didn't even mention it. We have to.' (*No*). Urrutia envisages a NO coalition, and Chile by extension, united in its victimisation by the brutal and unjust military regime of the last fifteen years. He believed that the shared memory of an immediate, violent past would lead to the forging of a communitarian identity characterised by a collective sense of victimhood. Therefore, the advertisement first proposed included visuals of a Chile ravaged by the brutality of Pinochet's human rights abuses and injustices – the crumbling edifice of the presidential palace bombed in 1973, numerous dead bodies sprawled on the streets and sidewalks, processions of military tanks and hundreds of soldiers, protesters brutally silenced by armed men, the statistics of the number of people tortured, exiled and executed – accompanied by a grim soundtrack. This advertisement, which was eventually rejected, envisioned a Chile united by its painful immediate past.

Both the YES and NO factions expected the NO campaign to promote an anti-Pinochet narrative. In the film, Lucho Guzman, the advisor for the YES campaign, assumes that their biggest challenge would be the job of making the dictator appealing to the public, 'the concept of dictatorship packs a strong punch. And on top of that, now they're going to say it on TV'. In order to pre-empt the attacks on Pinochet, the YES camp gets him out of his uniform and military trappings and into a suit that will complement 'his blue eyes, his smile.' The advertisement that Saavedra and his crew eventually put together for the NO camp rejects the narrative trajectory that the NO campaign was expected to take by both the factions.

The YES and NO campaigns were both aired in the form of fifteen-minute-long daily news shows, wherein a news reader took the audience through the various arguments put forward by each faction in the form of different segments. The first advertisement for the NO campaign was presented by the anchor as a news bulletin: 'Chile, happiness is coming. Good evening. For the first time in fifteen years, those who don't share the official point of view are talking to you through their own TV show. . . . Fifteen minutes in fifteen years isn't much. Let's talk about the coming happiness.' This was followed by a fantastic narrative constituted by visuals of children playing, families picnicking, people of all ages and from all walks of life smiling, laughing or dancing on the streets of Chile with reckless abandon, while singing 'We're going to say no.' These visuals were accompanied by a catchy jingle with the refrain, 'Chile, happiness is on its way' playing in the background (*No*). The fifteen minutes that seemed barely enough to showcase the grievances of the Chilean people that had been suppressed for the past fifteen years were instead used to present to the public a prospective Chile. The actual past was disnarrated in favour of an imagined future. Moreover, this counterfactual narrative delivered through the realistic medium of a TV news report constituted a disnarration of generic expectations. The format of a news report was evoked with the attendant expectations of narratives steeped in facts and figures, alluding to an authentic lived experience, only to be discarded in favour of a narrative of Chile that is nothing short of fantastic. The news report is even prefaced by the uncharacteristic prophetic declaration, 'Chile, happiness is coming'.

A Campaign of Silence

The counterintuitive shift in the campaign's focus from Chile's painful past to the happiness of an imagined future disorients the YES camp and, at the same time, infuriates some of the politicians of the NO camp who consider it 'a campaign to silence what ha[d] really happened' (*No*). As Reed Johnson observes in an article that appeared in the 9 Feb 2013 issue of the *Los Angeles Times*, 'what made the "No" campaign radically subversive and highly controversial, even among its supporters, was that it often avoided mentioning politics or Pinochet directly.' On a similar note, in a study published on Chile, as part of the Country Studies/ Area Handbook Series sponsored by the U.S. Department of the Army between 1986 and 1998, Arturo Valenzuela remarks that the NO campaign only 'hinted at the poverty and oppression average people had suffered under the dictatorship'.

To those who objected to the ahistorical narrative conceived by Saavedra, the NO advertisements' indifference to the crimes of the regime was an unpardonable betrayal of the legacy of resistance of the Chilean people. One politician from this group of dissenters proclaims that a campaign built on Saavedra's vision would be 'a campaign of silence'. Their anger towards this 'blasphemous', unrealistic narrative of Chile and their comparison of it to a Coca-Cola commercial (*No*) reinforces an axiom of nation formation that follows from Anderson's theorisation of nation as an 'imagined' community – the concealment of the rhetorical mechanics aiding nation formation. Though a similar rhetoric of persuasion underlies both a commercial narrative and a national narrative, it is in the interest of nation formation to underplay the fact that the 'nation' is an idea sold to the populace through narratives. The real/rhetorical divide evoked by these politicians in the film can be interpreted as an attempt to understate the rhetorical aspect of bringing a nation into narration. The emphasis on such a divide seems to imply that national narratives do not need to resort to contrivances (of the kind that characterise commercial ones) because their veracity speaks for them.

The internal dissent in the NO camp owing to the campaign's apparent neglect of Chile's suffering under the brutal regime is accompanied by two further instances wherein the accuracy of the campaign's representation of Chilean identity is questioned. In the first instance, Fernando Arancibia, the director of the advertisements, finds the presence of baguettes at the Chilean family picnic scene he was shooting quite anomalous: 'Get me some homemade bread . . . no one eats baguettes here' (*No*). Though the scene is eventually shot with the baguettes, Arancibia expresses his displeasure with it through his remark that the Chilean picnic was devoid of identity.

In the second instance, Saavedra's estranged wife angrily describes the NO advertisement as a vapid 'copy of a copy of a copy of a copy . . . .' Like the politician who insinuated that the NO campaign was 'a campaign of silence', Saavedra's wife contemptuously berates the decontextual, apolitical, ahistorical nature of the recurring campaign advertisement: 'You mixed rainbows, pretty people, blonde children skipping, celebrating I-don't-know-what. A tall man who's 15 feet tall. Where did you find him? Denmark? Who is that guy? Us Chileans are small. Who are all these people laughing, celebrating? Celebrating what?' (*No*). And, yet, this unspecific, universalist message with its empty signifiers did capture the national imagination. The gap between what was expected and what is said/shown can be negotiated with the help of 'relevance theory,' first proposed by Dan Sperber and Deirdre Wilson in *Relevance: Communication and Cognition* (1986), and revised and republished repeatedly before being compiled in *The Handbook of Pragmatics* (2004).

National Narratives and 'Relevance'

The relevance-theoretical model is a highly effective methodological framework employed in the field of narrative pragmatics[7], that is, the study of the part played by contextual factors in determining the efficacy of communication. According to this theory, any utterance raises expectations of relevance, and the individual at the receiving end of the communication processes the utterance in such a manner as to maximise its relevance to him/her. Here, the term 'relevance' indicates 'a measure of cognitive benefit' (Walsh 157). To paraphrase Sperber and Wilson, an input (that is, a sight, a sound or an utterance) is relevant to an individual if, upon being processed in a context of facts known and assumptions available to the individual at that particular time, it yields positive cognitive effects: 'Other things being equal, an assumption with greater contextual effects is more relevant; and, other things being equal, an assumption requiring a smaller processing effort is more relevant' (*Relevance* 125).

The 'cognitive principle of relevance'[8] proposed by Sperber and Wilson aids communicators to 'produce a stimulus[9] which is likely to attract [the audience's] attention, to prompt the retrieval of certain contextual assumptions and point [it] towards an intended conclusion' ('Relevance Theory', 611). This knowledge is highly necessary for communicating via advertisements which are essentially commercial bulletins bound by time constraints that vie with one another for the audience's attention. The advertising discourse operates via a rhetoric of persuasion wherein 'the propositional criterion of truth is a subordinate consideration to the contextual pragmatic criterion of relevance' (Walsh 156). A relevance-theoretical analysis of the historically moored anti-Pinochet narrative that was first proposed as the theme of the NO campaign and the fantastic utopian narrative that was finally broadcast as the official NO advertisement will hopefully delineate the efficacy of the latter in mobilising the citizens to vote 'No'.

The historically-moored narrative was intended as an exposé of the military regime's brutality and a medium through which to air the public's grievances against the Pinochet government. The explicit premise[10] of this narrative is that 'the Pinochet government was unjust and brutal,' the implicit premise[11] is that 'if Pinochet comes to power again, violence will continue' and the implicit conclusion is that 'I should not vote Yes'. By bombarding the audience with visuals of the violence perpetrated by the regime, the advertisement is likely to intensify the public's fear of the regime and its mistrust of the legitimacy of the plebiscite, and thereby prove counterproductive[12]. The risk of the communication going awry is high in this case. The advertisement's reiteration of the regime's violence coupled with the people's belief that the result of this referendum might also be manipulated by the government similar to the result of the 1980 referendum was likely to result in their abstention from voting. Therefore, such an advertisement offered little incentive for the audience to vote 'No'. In relevance-theoretic terms, this advertisement would not have radically altered the audience's cognitive environment.

Saavedra's utopian narrative, on the other hand, addressed the question, 'Why vote No?'. The slogan 'Chile, happiness is on its way' accompanied by visuals of unencumbered, happy people dancing and humming the words of the jingle out in the streets created in the audience a positive effect that was juxtaposed with their present condition and thus reinforced. The explicature of this narrative is that 'happiness is on its way to Chile' and the implicature is that 'the emotion of happiness is absent from Chile at present.' The communicator co-opts the audience here by establishing a shared frame of reference with the recipient, the current repressive political climate. This shared frame of reference makes available to the audience the assumption that the Pinochet regime is responsible for the absence of joy in Chile. This assumption emerges in the public imagination as a weak implicature which, together with the implicit premise first recovered, helps the audience arrive at the implicit conclusion that 'Chile could attain happiness again by saying "No" to Pinochet.' Saavedra's ahistorical vision addresses itself to an intelligent audience by disnarrating the shared past in his narrative of a utopian future. The disnarrated past offers the necessary contrast to Saavedra's fantastic narrative, thus strengthening the implicit conclusion of the latter. This spectral narrative emerges as a weak implicature of the ahistorical advertisement, thereby allaying fears of 'paradoxical imagining' and censorship.

As depicted in the film, only one of the twenty-seven television slots for the 'No' vote was censored throughout the duration of campaigning. The theme for that particular slot was the regime's torture of dissidents. Paula Cronovich documents that 'on September 12, 1988, the program opens with the message: "This program was censored" across the screen.' The government had refused to allow a judge to appear on that particular slot to share with the public his knowledge of its unequivocal involvement in over fifty cases of torture. This move by the government proved to be counterproductive. Mere absence of speech or auditory signals is not silence, but the absence of expected speech or auditory signals is: '[the] phenomenological existence [of silence] depends on somebody's perception that something is missing' (Schröter 23). Therefore, the silence in this case – foregrounded by the time 'frame' of the campaign slot – became an 'ostensive stimulus' aiding the public in recovering the explicature (the absence of expected communication) and the implicature (the censored information probably had the potential to debilitate the government) to arrive at the implicit conclusion that the censorship pointed to the government's acknowledgement of its culpability.

The NO campaign utilised the televisual slots allotted to it through a careful negotiation of the speech/silence dichotomy. The campaign's disnarration of Chile's torturous past at the hands of the military regime led the dissenters within the NO faction to dub it 'a campaign of silence' due to a misperception of 'semantic[ally] and/or logical[ly] empty slots . . . such as presupposition . . . implicature . . . connotation and allusion' (Schröter 17) as silence. As a relevance-theoretic analysis of the NO campaign's political communiqué reveals, this is hardly the case. Both the intentional silence of the NO campaign, maintained via the disnarration of Chile's immediate past, and the silence imposed on it through government censorship thus prove to be communicative.

Nation vis-à-vis 'Desired Worlds'

Ernst Renan was among the first to remark that the idea that 'nation' is constituted by such empirical categories as race, language or geography is a popular misconception, pointing out instead that it is constituted by 'a rich legacy of memories' and 'the desire to live together' (19). What Renan identified in his lecture as a popular misconception is, in fact, a deliberate denial of the truth of the immateriality of 'nation'. That 'nation' is merely the product of ideation is a statement that is received with tacit acceptance today, at least in the intellectual circles. National narratives attempt to disguise this by attributing to 'nation,' among other things, historicity in order to plant it firmly outside the realm of abstractions and desires.

In the film *No*, as with the original campaign, the possibility of a historical national narrative is evoked but not pursued. What is pursued in its stead is what usually belongs to the category of 'purely imagined worlds, desired worlds, or intended worlds, [and] unfulfilled expectations . . .' (Prince, 'The Disnarrated', 32). Traditional historically-moored national narratives choose to disnarrate, or rather, render unnarratable the 'desired' and 'imagined' quality of nations to further their project. Saavedra's narrative, on the contrary, rejects a historical trajectory in order to market a hypothetical, desirable nation unencumbered by the baggage of history. Saavedra literally sells the idea of nationhood to a public by appealing to human desire, perhaps the oldest and most effective trick in any advertising executive's bag. Saavedra's narrative appeals to the Chilean public's 'desire' to sustain its collective identity, identified by Renan as one of the building blocks of the modern nation. But, it does so by openly flaunting the rhetorical mechanics employed to foster such a desire.

Disnarration offers a metanarratorial comment on the process of narration itself by drawing our attention to the mechanics underlying it: 'every narrative progresses by following certain directions as opposed to others . . .' (Prince, 'The Disnarrated', 36). In its disnarration of the past, an integral ingredient of national narratives, Saavedra's narrative can be read as a meta-commentary on the mechanics of national narratives. Through a relevance-theoretic analysis of both the advertisements, I have hazarded an explanation for Saavedra's rejection of the historically-moored narrative first proposed.

In conclusion, I dwell very briefly on certain disturbing implications of the acceptance of this utopian narrative by the Chilean public. The revolutionary nature of the campaign, while hailed by Larraín, is not spared from critique owing to its capitalistic foundation:

> Pinochet wasn't defeated through a political revolution, but by a neoliberalist way of looking at life: marketing. We're talking

> about people who sell spaghetti, we're not talking about Che Guevara. For me, the movie's not just about what happened before the referendum, it's about what happened after. Since 1988, we've been living in a shopping centre. *No* is not just about defeating Pinochet, it's about where Chile is going – and what's going on now is terrible. (Larraín, qtd. in Romney 32)

Ultimately, Rene Saavedra is an advertising executive. He uses the same sales pitch[13] to sell a soft drink, a Pinochet-free Chile and a soap opera. In the end, Pinochet is defeated by the by-products of the neo-liberal reforms he introduced into Chile. Larraín's focus on the thematic of 'marketing' is underscored by his choice of the advertising executive as the protagonist through whose point of view the narrative unfolds. Through Saavedra, Larraín offers a rather cynical examination of advertising mechanics and semiology.

Saavedra's narrative speaks the universal language of capital and not the language of nationalism based on a shared past, or on the Chilean population's lived experience of victimhood under the military regime. While it exposes the mechanics of national narratives by drawing an unintentional comparison between nationalism and marketing, it also offers a disturbing glimpse into consumerism's potent hold over the collective global psyche. Saavedra's fantastic narrative, with its attempt to sell an abstraction like 'happiness' to the Chilean public, seems to appeal more to the citizens' 'desire to live together' as consumers. The victory of this particular national narrative offers an unwitting prognostication of a future in which communitarian identities with far more harrowing consequences might be fashioned.

Notes

1. Provisions for the 1988 plebiscite to determine Pinochet's continuation in office were outlined in the constitution drawn up by the military government in 1980 in a move to legalise its reforms and legitimise its tenure. This constitution was ratified through a controlled, fraudulent plebiscite in which the government claimed to have received 67 per cent of the votes in favour of the new constitution. Absence of any security for the opposition or for the

balloting led to suspicion among dissidents and political analysts as to the authenticity of the referendum (Drake).

2. Under the military dictatorship, the Chilean population was subjected to some of the worst human rights abuses in history, with hundreds of thousands of civilians 'murdered, jailed, tortured, brutalized, or exiled, especially those linked with the Popular Unity parties. The secret police, reporting to Pinochet through the National Intelligence Directorate (Dirección Nacional de Inteligencia – DINA), replaced in 1977 by the National Information Center (Centro Nacional de Información – CNI), kept dissidents living in fear of arrest, torture, murder, or "disappearance" '(Drake).
3. The accuracy of Larraín's fictionalised portrayal of the differences in the NO coalition members' political opinions, campaigning techniques and attitudes towards the referendum is attested by the scant non-fictional accounts of the 1988 referendum accessible to the Anglophone world. 'The "NO" Campaign in Chile: Paving a Peaceful Transition to Democracy', a conference paper presented at the twelfth annual *Conversation on the Liberal Arts* conducted by Gaede Institute for the Liberal Arts in February 2013, alludes to these differences. This paper also helpfully lists out the few secondary resources available on the NO campaign in Spanish. For a concise introduction to the political landscape in Chile prior to the plebiscite, particularly in the months leading up to it, refer to Alexander Hopkins' article, ' "Pressing Disengagement:" Chile's Transition to Democracy after Augusto Pinochet's 1973 Military Coup.' Also, see 'How advertising brought down a dictator', published in January 2013, in *Campaign*, a leading magazine on advertising and the commercial media industry published in the UK, for Larrain's commentary on the film and the historical milestone in Chilean history that inspired it.
4. Many historians identify the act of remembering to be indispensable to the fashioning of agenda-driven identitarian narratives. The act of recalling a nation's past involves not a simple recollection but a reconstruction of its history in the interest of the present and the future. In *Voices of Collective Remembering*, Wertsch argues that in periods of uncertainty in a nation's history, a community invokes its 'collective memory' as an 'identity resource' for plotting narratives of heroism or victimhood geared towards the creation of a 'usable past' (69, 95–96).

5. My access to the polispots is limited to those segments of the TV campaigns embedded in and framed by the film's narrative. Since Mr Larraín himself has remarked that 'about 30 per cent of the film' uses documentary footage from the original campaigns shot in 1988 (Rohter), and because the particular segments from the TV campaigns that I discuss in detail in this paper appear enclosed in full within the film's narrative, I will not be citing the campaign advertisements separately.
6. According to Anderson, nations 'loom out of an immemorial past, and . . . glide into a limitless future' (11–12).
7. According to Gerald Prince, 'narrative pragmatics specifies the cognitive and communicative factors affecting the processing, tellability, suitability, and value of narratives. . . . '('Narrative Pragmatics', 529).
8. According to this, 'human cognition tends to be geared to the maximization of relevance' (*Relevance,* 261).
9. Sperber and Wilson qualify such a stimulus as an 'ostensive stimulus', that conveys a presumption of its relevance and makes manifest the communicative intention of the speaker to the listener ('Relevance Theory', 256).
10. The 'explicature' in relevance-theoretic terms. The explicature is the explicitly communicated meaning of an input which forms the premise on the basis of which contextual implications are derived.
11. The 'implicature' in relevance-theoretic terms. The implicature is that which is suggested but not explicitly expressed. It is discerned by the listener on the basis of the explicature with the aid of facts known and assumptions available to him/her. These facts and assumptions already available to the listener constitute the context within which s/he processes the input.
12. Sakari Katajamäki uses the term 'paradoxical imagining' (qtd in Karttunen 438) to refer to the human tendency to conjure strong mental imprints of negative imagery in literature and media, thus triggering negative associations with them. On a similar vein, Cronovich observes that 'the hitch with political communication is that people identify the image with the transmitter.'
13. In the film's opening sequence, before introducing a soft-drink commercial to his clients, Saavedra remarks: 'First of all, I'd like to say that what you're about to see fits with the current social context. We believe the country is ready for communication like this. Remember, the citizens have increased demands about the

truth, and what they want. Let's be honest, today, Chile is thinking of its future.' He uses a variation of the same prefatory speech while introducing the first draft of the advertisement for the NO campaign to the coalition.

WORKS CITED

Anderson, Benedict. *Imagined Communities: Reflections on the Origin and Spread of Nationalism*. London: Verso, 2006. Print.

Cronovich, Paula. 'The "No" Campaign in Chile: Paving a Peaceful Transition to Democracy.' *War and Peace as Liberal Arts: The Twelfth Annual Conversation on the Liberal Arts*. Gaede Institute for the Liberal Arts, Santa Barbara: Feb. 2013. *Gaede Institute for the Liberal Arts*. Web. 17 Feb. 2014.

Drake, Paul W. 'Historical Setting.' *Chile: A Country Study*. Ed. Rex A. Hudson. Washington: GPO for the Library of Congress, 1994. N. pag. *Country Studies*. Web. 29 Jan. 2014.

Hopkins, Alexander E. ' "Pressing Disengagement:" Chile's Transition to Democracy After Augusto Pinochet's 1973 Military Coup.' *Student Pulse* 4.9 (2012): 0. Web. 19 Jan. 2014.

Johnson, Reed. ' "No" Finds Gael Garcia Bernal Campaigning against Pinochet.' *Los Angeles Times*, 09 Feb. 2013. Web. 16 Jan. 2014.

Karttunen, Laura. 'A Sociostylistic Perspective on Negatives and the Disnarrated: Lahiri, Roy, Rushdie.' *Partial Answers: Journal of Literature and the History of Ideas* 6.2 (2008): 419–41. *Project Muse*. Web. 12 Jan. 2014.

Larraín, Pablo. 'How Advertising Brought down a Dictator.' *Campaign*. 17 Jan. 2013. Web. 26 Feb. 2014.

No. Dir. Pablo Larraín. Perf. Gael García Bernal, Alfredo Castro, Antonia Zegers. Participant Media, 2012. Film.

Prince, Gerald. 'The Disnarrated.' *Narrative as Theme: Studies in French Fiction*. Lincoln: U of Nebraska, 1992. 28–38. Print.

———. 'Narrative Pragmatics, Message, and Point.' *Poetics* 12 (1983): 527–36. *ScienceDirect*. Web. 10 Mar. 2014.

Renan, Ernest. 'What Is a Nation?' In *Nation and Narration*. Ed. Homi K. Bhabha. London: Routledge, 1990. 8–22. Print.

Rohter, Larry. 'One Prism on the Undoing of Pinochet.' *New York Times*. New York Times, 09 Feb. 2013. Web. 7 Mar. 2014.

Romney, Jonathan. 'The Future Is No.' *Sight and Sound*. Mar. 2013: 28–32. Print.

Schröter, Melani. 'Intention, Expectation and Relevance: Determinants of Meaningful Silence.' *Silence and Concealment in Political Discourse*. Philadelphia: John Benjamins, 2013. 13–42. Print. Discourse Approaches to Politics, Society and Culture 48.

Sperber, Dan, and Deirdre Wilson. *Relevance: Communication and Cognition*. Cambridge (Mass.): Blackwell Publishing, 1995. Print.

———. 'Relevance Theory.' *The Handbook of Pragmatics*. Ed. Laurence R. Horn and Gregory L. Ward. Malden, MA: Blackwell Publishing, 2004. 607–32. Print.

Valenzuela, Arturo. 'Government and Politics.' *Chile: A Country Study*. Ed. Rex A. Hudson. Washington: GPO for the Library of Congress, 1994. N. pag. *Country Studies*. Web. 29 Jan. 2014.

Walsh, Richard. 'The Pragmatics of Narrative Fictionality.' *A Companion to Narrative Theory*. Ed. James Phelan and Peter J. Rabinowitz. Malden, MA: Blackwell Publishing, 2005. 150–64. Print.

Wertsch, James V. *Voices of Collective Remembering*. Cambridge, U.K.: Cambridge UP, 2002. Print.

The Contributors

Supriya Chaudhuri was educated at Kolkata and Oxford and is Professor (Emerita) in the Department of English, Jadavpur University, Kolkata, having served as Departmental Chair and Coordinator of its Centre of Advanced Study. Her specialisations include European Renaissance literature, 19th and early 20th century cultural history, modernism, narrative, critical theory and sport. Among her recent publications, some co-authored, some co-edited, are *Reconsidering English Studies in Indian Higher Education; Sport, Literature, Society: Cultural Historical Studies; Petrarch: the Self and the World,* and *Conversations with Jacqueline Rose.* She has contributed chapters to *A Companion to Virginia Woolf*; *A History of the Indian Novel in English; Celebrating Shakespeare; Renaissance Shakespeare, Shakespeare Renaissances; The Cambridge Companion to Modern Indian Culture*, and *The Oxford Handbook of Modernisms.* She has translated Bangla modernist poetry as well as the poetry and fiction of Rabindranath Tagore for the *Oxford Tagore Translations* series and *The Essential Tagore.*

Jasbir Jain has worked in a wide range of areas. Former Sahitya Akademi Writer-in-Residence (University of Rajasthan), she has also been an Emeritus Fellow and a K.K. Birla Fellow in Comparative Literature. Recipient of the 2008 SALA Award for distinguished scholarship and the 2003 IACS award for lifetime achievement, Jain has written extensively on cultural and literary issues with a special focus on narratology, gender and Indian literatures. Amongst her most recent publications are *Beyond Postcolonialism: The Dreams and Realities of a Nation; Indigenous Roots of Feminism: Culture, Subjectivity and Agency; Theorizing Resistance,* and *The Diaspora Writes Home.* She is currently working on the areas of postcoloniality, subalternity and their limitations.

Debapriya Basu is Assistant Professor in the Department of Humanities and Social Sciences, IIT Guwahati. Her research is on the writings of Renaissance Englishwomen on which she has published extensively. She has worked at the School of Cultural Texts and Records (SCTR), Jadavpur University, as Research Fellow, and has taught in the SCTR's Postgraduate Diploma Course in Digital Humanities and Cultural Informatics. She was Project Supervisor in the Bichitra Tagore Online Variorum project (www.bichitra.jdvu.ac.in) and is a contributor in *Bichitra: The Making of an Online Tagore Variorum,* edited by Sukanta Chaudhuri. Her postdoctoral work is the creation of an electronic edition of the works of the English Protestant martyr Anne Askew, funded by an Erasmus Mundus fellowship to the University of Amsterdam. This edition is available at www.anne-askew.humanities.uva.nl.

Paulomi Chakraborty is Assistant Professor of English in the Department of Humanities and Social Sciences in IIT Bombay. Her publications include a research article in *English Studies in Canada,* a chapter in *Partitioned Lives: Narratives of Home, Displacement, and Resettlement,* edited by Anjali Gera Roy and Nandi Bhatia, and book reviews in *Canadian Literature: A Quarterly of Criticism and Review* and *Economic and Political Weekly.* She has, by invitation, also contributed book chapters to *Routledge Handbook on Gender in South Asia,* edited by Leela Fernandes, and *Being Bengali: At Home and in the World,* edited by Mridula Chakraborty. At this moment, she is finalising a book manuscript tentatively titled *The Refugee Woman: Partition of Bengal, Gender, and the Political.* Her research interests are gender-focused and in the Partition of 1947, the turbulent '40s in Bengal, and cultures of the political left.

Shinjini Chattopadhyay is a second year MPhil research scholar at the Department of English, Jadavpur University. She is writing her MPhil dissertation on James Joyce. She has obtained her Bachelors' and Masters' degrees from the same department. She is also a faculty member at the West Bengal National University of Juridical Sciences, Kolkata. She has presented papers at the 2013 annual conference of the American Association for Australasian Literary Studies at Georgetown University, where she won the Wertheim Prize for the best graduate student paper; at the 2015 Literary London Conference, hosted by the University of London, and at several other national and international conferences. Her areas of interest include any form of modernist art and literature.

Sreya Dutt is pursuing her PhD degree at the Department of Film Studies, Jadavpur University. She is working on the aesthetics of violence in film and other narrative forms related to the Kashmir conflict. She is also Contractual Whole Time Teacher in the Postgraduate Department of English, Basanti Devi College, Kolkata.

Rohit Dutta Roy is a research scholar at the Centre for Historical Studies, Jawaharlal Nehru University, Delhi, having done his BA and MA degrees in comparative literature from Jadavpur University, and another MA in history from the University of Delhi. He has been reviews editor for *Inquire: Journal of Comparative Literature* and is currently reviews editor with the *Journal of Studies in History and Culture*. He has presented his scholarly work at the Jawaharlal Nehru University, University of Delhi, Aligarh Muslim University, IIT Bombay, Duke University, University of Cambridge, Brown University and Columbia University. His present research work traces the evolution of historical writing in a positivist mould in early twentieth-century Bengal, while analysing the wide-ranging influences on the same. His interest areas include interdisciplinary studies, secularisation in comparative political theory, and the transactions between the proscenium and the traditional Indian theatre.

David Jeyaraj Franklin. T is Assistant Professor of English at the Gandhigram Rural Institute – Deemed University, Gandhigram, Tamil Nadu. He teaches courses on English language and literature to graduate and postgraduate students at Gandhigram. He has been teaching for the last ten years. He has presented papers and published articles on theory, ecocriticism, and native literatures. He is currently pursuing his doctoral research on native/indigenous fiction from around the world and that list includes Kim Scott, Louise Erdrich, 'Kocharethi' Narayan, Ngugi wa Thiongo, Jose Maria Arguedas, and Bernardo Atxaga. This research would focus on the literary representations of native issues from the 20th century. He is fond of indiscriminate reading and follows cricket and Formula 1.

Anushka Sen has received her BA and MA degrees in English from Jadavpur University. She has worked on an urban studies project under the School of Media Communication and Culture at Jadavpur University. Her literary interests include modernism, Shakespeare, and poetry of all sorts. Some of her favourites are J.M. Coetzee,

Vladmir Nabokov and Seamus Heaney. She has also published a paper on Kazuo Ishiguro in the journal *Sanglap*. She is interested in feminism, animal welfare and children's education, and hopes to contribute increasingly to each of these fields.

Vinita Singh is an MPhil scholar from the Department of English, University of Delhi. Her dissertation was titled 'The Politics of Sexuality and the Disabled Body in India.' Her area of interest is disability studies, human rights, health and sexuality.

Krishnan Unni. P is Associate Professor in English at Deshbandhu College in Delhi University. He has edited a book on Gabriel Garcia Marquez's *Chronicle of a Death Foretold* and authored a book of essays and a collection of poems in Malayalam. He is a creative writer in English and Malayalam and his work has appeared in national and international journals and magazines. He has presented papers in the University of Nottingham, Cairo University, University at Lund, Sweden, the National University of Brussels and at several other universities in India. He is a Board of Studies member in the University of Kashmir, Srinagar and is a nominated member in the Culture Studies department in Cairo University. His areas of interests are Third World literatures and films, gender discourse, changing patterns of sexual dissidence and the politics of the dispossessed – in relation to music, football and popular culture.

Nisha Viswanathan is a doctoral research scholar in the Department of Humanities and Social Sciences at IIT Bombay. She has an MA and MPhil in English from the University of Hyderabad. Her MPhil dissertation, 'Of Vampires and Virgules: The Twenty-First Century Literary Vampire as a Critical Posthumanist Trope', is a study of the re-appropriation of the vampire myth in the age of technoscience. This project borrows theoretical approaches from the disciplines of cultural studies, gender studies, animal studies and technoscience studies to question the prevailing anthropocentric world view. Her current research examines the expatriate Chilean writer Roberto Bolaño's fiction in translation, with particular attention to its metaliterary concerns. She is currently engaged in an inquiry into the metaphysics of fiction impelled by her encounter with Bolaño's oeuvre, focusing on his experiments with narrative and form. She has presented papers in national and international conferences at home and abroad.